ENDS OF THE EARTH
THE WORLD'S REMOTE AND WILD PLACES

The Kalahari

Rose Inserra and Susan Powell

Heinemann
LIBRARY

© 1997 Rose Inserra and Susan Powell

Published by Heinemann Library

an imprint of Reed Educational & Professional Publishing

500 Coventry Lane

Crystal Lake, IL 60014

Library of Congress Cataloging-in-Publication Data

Inserra, Rose, 1958-

    The Kalahari / Rose Insera and Susan Powell.

      p. cm. -- (Ends of the earth)

    Includes index.

    ISBN 0-431-06932-8 (lib. bind.)

    1. Kalahari Desert--Juvenile literature. 2. Natural History--Kalahari Desert--

Juvenile literature 3. Nature--Effect of human beings on--Kalahari Desert--

Juvenile literature. I. Powell, Susan, 1942- . II. Title. III. Series.

DT1190.K35155 1997

916.883--dc21

                         96-54863

                           CIP

                            AC

01 00 99 98 97

10 9 8 7 6 5 4 3 2 1

Designed by David Doyle and Irwin Liaw

Edited by Ogma Writers and Editors

Front cover photograph courtesy of Peter Lemon, Peregrine Adventure

Back cover photograph courtesy of The African Wildlife Safari Co.

Picture research by Ogma Writers and Editors

Cartography by Ophelia Leviny, Anita Belia, David Doyle

Production by Elena Cementon

Printed in Hong Kong by H&Y Printing Limited

Contents

The Kalahari

The Kalahari, semi-arid and without streams and rivers, is very different from the Okavango Delta. Yet, both are valuable natural resources and both can be sensitive to misuse. Both could be destroyed through ignorance, haste, or greed. It is our privilege to use them, but it is our duty to conserve them for the future.

Dr Quett Masire, President of Botswana

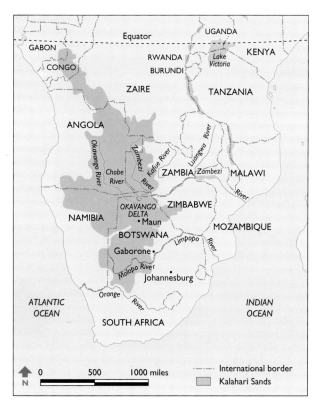

Figure 1 The Kalahari stretches from the Congo in the north through Angola, Zambia, Namibia and Botswana, and into South Africa.

The Kalahari Desert, in southern Africa, is a place that is so vast, mysterious, and ancient that the unique people who live there call it *Kgalagadi*, meaning "wilderness." It covers almost all of Botswana, reaches west into Namibia, and stretches north into Angola, Zambia, and Zimbabwe.

Unlike the lush tropical rainforests of the world, the Kalahari does not automatically appeal to our idea of beauty. It contains vast areas of coarse red sand and sparse dry vegetation, and the relentless heat is at times beyond human endurance. The eroded, windswept landscape seems to stretch across a monotonous flat plain of browns and yellows.

The largest area of the Kalahari is the huge sand-filled basin at its center. In the northern part of the wilderness is an oasis beyond imagination called the Okavango Delta—the jewel in the crown of the Kalahari. Further east are enormous salt crystal lakes. When the rains come, the lakes overflow to form hundreds of small "islands."

The Kalahari contains a wonderful variety of animals that are uniquely adapted to survive in their environment. Among the people who populate the region are the Kalahari Bushmen, some of whom continue their unique traditional way of life today.

Figure 2 (right)   The Kalahari region.

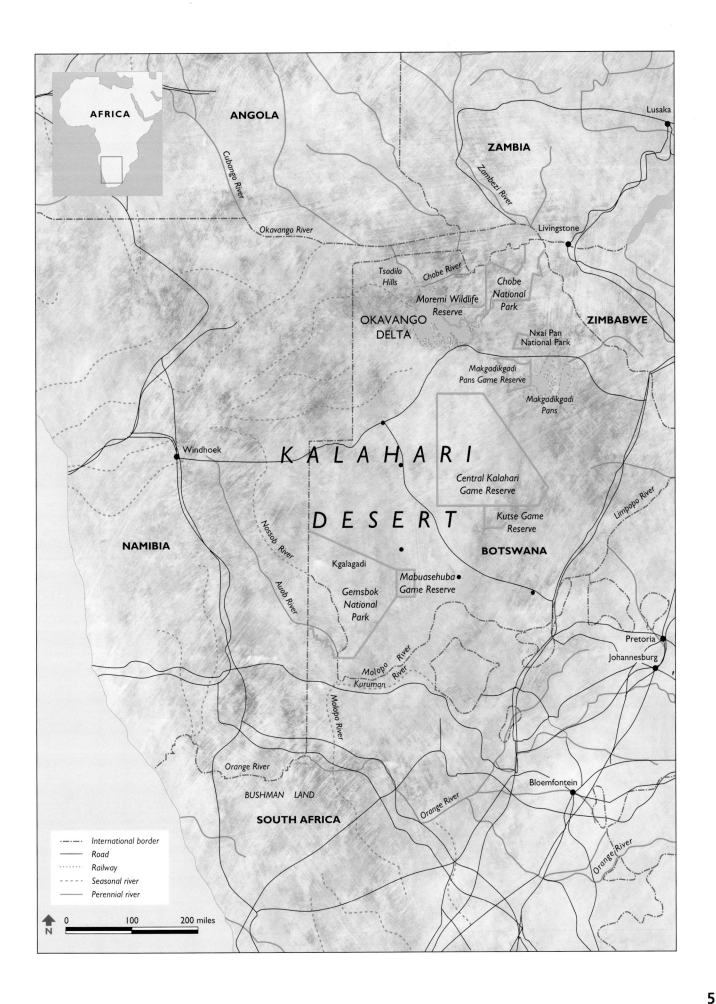

Birth of the Kalahari

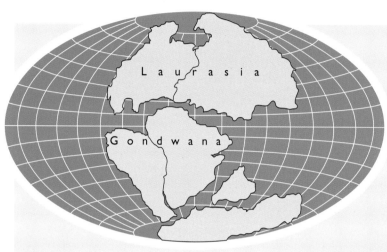

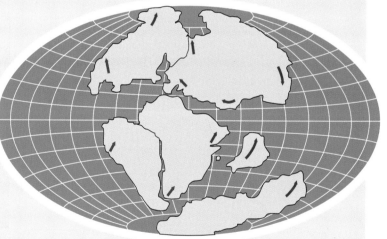

Figure 3a (left)   **180 million years ago**

Figure 3b (right)   **135 million years ago**
The beginning of the Kalahari goes back to when the southern part of the supercontinent of Gondwana was beginning to break up. It was an age when the only mammals were tiny nocturnal creatures, hiding from the dinosaurs that roamed the giant continent.

India and Madagascar were the first to cut their connection from Gondwana. Then Antarctica and Australia broke away from the southeastern side. A million years later South America broke off from the western side and began to move slowly away.

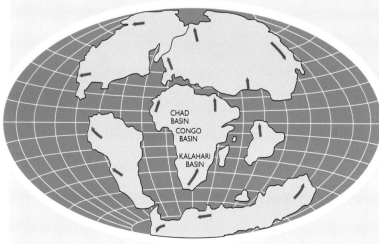

Figure 3c (left)   **100 million years ago**
Africa stood alone as a continent. In the interior, three huge basins were formed— the Chad, the Congo, and the Kalahari.

65 million years ago
More movements shaped the continent. Massive convulsions shook the Earth, and volcanic lava spewed out over central southern Africa. These seas of lava, up to 5 miles deep in some places, formed high ridges and deep river valleys.

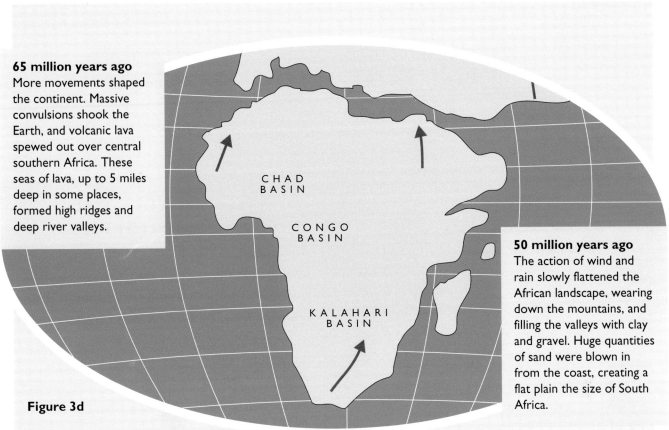

CHAD BASIN

CONGO BASIN

KALAHARI BASIN

Figure 3d

50 million years ago
The action of wind and rain slowly flattened the African landscape, wearing down the mountains, and filling the valleys with clay and gravel. Huge quantities of sand were blown in from the coast, creating a flat plain the size of South Africa.

5 million years ago
The climate of the Kalahari became drier as Antarctica moved closer to the South Pole. The cold sea currents and air flows that froze Antarctica sucked up the moisture in the south of the African continent. The lush, subtropical climate of the Kalahari gave way to extremely dry, drought conditions. It was during this time that plants and animals evolved their extraordinary adaptations to their new environment.

Okavango delta

Lake Makgadikgadi

Figure 3e

3 million years ago
The climate was now at its driest, and the Kalahari was very arid. Strong easterly winds blew the sands into long dunes from east to west, running in parallel lines across the central Kalahari. These dunes changed the flow of the rivers in the wet season, and the Kalahari sands formed one of the largest lakes in Africa, Lake Makgadikgadi. The Okavango Delta of today is the last remaining part of this ancient lake, and a reminder that the Kalahari was once a region of subtropical rainforests, rivers, and lakes.

The Kalahari today

The landscape of the Kalahari has not changed greatly since the last great "drying-out" period. The sand dunes are now stabilized by vegetation. The troughs between the ridges of these dunes form winding river valleys called "fossil valleys" because they are remains of ancient rivers which once carried huge volumes of water across the Kalahari. Now they act as drainage channels for the water that collects during the rains. For most of the year, however, water can only be found underground.

Although many consider the Kalahari a desert, its varied landscape and unpredictable rainfall mean that much of the region contains life both on the surface and underground. In the northern part of the Kalahari, toward Zaire, the rainfall exceeds 40 inches a year; in the far south it is less than half an inch. These extremes create an amazing contrast of landforms—from semi-desert to lush tropical forest.

The sands of the Kalahari

The closest to true desert conditions are found in southwest Botswana, northern South Africa, and southeast Namibia. Even in these areas the annual rainfall in some years is around 6 inches, so it is more accurate to call them arid rather than desert. The ancient sand dunes may stretch as far as the eye can see, but there are also extensive areas covered with grasses, shrubs, and trees. In some years when the rains are heavy, the landscape becomes a blanket of different shades of green. This burst of new life is short-lived as all the moisture from the rain either evaporates or is absorbed by the sand or the vegetation.

The seasons in the Kalahari fall into three distinct phases—the rains (December to March, April or May), the cold–dry season (June to August), and the hot–dry season (September to early December). In "summer" the temperature can soar above 120°F. In the rainy season the temperatures are not as high because the rain-soaked ground takes longer to heat up. The cold season temperatures can drop to a freezing 25°F, and a light snow cover has been reported in some areas. The animal and plant life of the Kalahari must be hardy in order to survive such a great variation in temperatures and rainfall.

(Photo courtesy of The African Wildlife Safari Co.)

Figure 4 (above)   One of the extremes of the Kalahari is this flat, hot desert, which looks as though it could support very little life.

(Photo courtesy of Greg Mortimer)

Figure 5 (above)   Africa's old neighbor, Antarctica, is responsible for the dryness of the Kalahari. The cold Benguela Current from the Antarctic flows past the west coast of southern Africa and chills the prevailing winds. In this chilled state, the winds cannot absorb moisture, and so do not bring the rain which would turn the wilderness into a green subtropical forest.

Kalahari's Witsands

Red sands are a common feature of the Kalahari, but in the southernmost point of the Kalahari sands, called the Witsands, there is an abrupt contrast. In the troughs between dunes measuring 160 to 200 feet high, there are large quantities of fresh water. More incredible still, the red sand gives way to coarse grains of white sand that rumble and thunder when walked upon. The sound that seems to come from deep inside the dune is like that of a passing truck and can be heard more than a third of a mile away. Scientists believe that the noise is due to the size of the white sand grains.

The grasslands

The central Kalahari is a sea of sun-dried grasses that partly cover the never-ending sand dunes. Among the savanna grasses are thorny thickets of acacias. Grasses are vital to life as their leaves and roots provide food and nesting material, and their seeds are eaten by insects, birds, and rodents. The grass dies each year because of winter frost, but its seeds are dispersed by the wind and quickly germinate with the arrival of rain.

Although the sand and soil in this central region are not very fertile, they are able to sustain life. The trees of the acacia group and various herbs are able to survive by supplying their own nitrogen fertilizer. Tiny organisms in their roots take nitrogen from the atmosphere and feed it to the plant. This enriches the soils and allows other types of grasses to grow.

(Photo courtesy of Peter Lemon, Peregrine Adventure)

Figure 6 Antelopes obtain extra minerals by chewing the bones of dead animals that have fallen victim to fierce predators or their deadliest enemy—drought.

Under the bleached grasslands is a very precious natural resource—underground water. However, there is disagreement about how much of this water can safely be used by drilling boreholes. Some people claim that the supply is not replenished, and once the water is gone there will be no more. Others believe that replenishment does take place and that there is an inexhaustible supply of water. The challenge is to understand the systems of ancient underground waterways, and determine how much water can be used safely without endangering the environment.

Further south, where four ancient dry rivers —the Molopo, Kuruman, Nossob, and Auob— meander toward the Orange River, water flows only in years of exceptional rain. Around these ghostly river beds, iron oxide has colored the sand grains various shades of copper and red. Deep below the ground, older river systems may be flowing, safe from the cruel Kalahari sun.

The pans of the Kalahari

Pans of salt, rock, and clay are scattered throughout the Kalahari. The Makgadikgadi Pans were once part of the ancient Lake Makgadikgadi, which stretched over 23,000 square miles. Around 10,000 years ago Lake Makgadikgadi began its drying-out process. As the lake continued to shrink, a series of smaller lakes

(Photo courtesy of The African Wildlife Safari Co.)

(Photo courtesy of Adventure World)

Figures 7 & 8 Wherever the rains fall, the animals of the Kalahari follow, to drink from the short-lived waterholes and channels, and to hunt in the grasslands.

formed but they, too, eventually disappeared. The only remaining permanent water body is the Okavango Delta. As the ancient lake grew smaller through evaporation, the salts within it became more concentrated. When it finally dried up, a hard crust of white salt formed on the former lake bed. No animals can live on the arid saltpans and nothing will grow there during the dry season.

However, a dramatic change takes place after the rains fill the pans. Desert succulents mysteriously appear and creatures such as tortoises, frogs, and tadpoles begin to inhabit the new water wonderland. Migratory herds of game follow the rains to the pans, attracting hyenas, jackals, cheetahs, and lions. Huge flocks of colorful flamingoes and waterfowl crowd the shallow water. The pans become the popular meeting place for an assortment of animals that are grateful for the abundance of precious water.

An inland delta

An oasis of plenty

Water is the most valuable treasure for people and animals in this arid landscape—it determines life and death. It is not surprising, then, that the most desirable place to be is near the Okavango Delta of the northern Kalahari—the world's largest inland delta (the size of Switzerland). It is made up of narrow waterways, swamps, and islands of emerald reed beds that bring life to the arid lands of the desert. Geologists call the Delta an alluvial fan because of the millions of tons of flood sediment that have been laid down there over millions of years. For the wildlife, it is an oasis of plenty, providing an abundance of food, water, and shelter.

The Delta's life begins in the Okavango River, which rises in the Angolan highlands and enters the Kalahari at the Botswana border. It is the scarcity of water that makes the river so precious to the inhabitants of the Kalahari. During dry periods, the Delta covers at least 6000 square miles, but in wetter years the Okavango waters can spread over 8500 square miles. It transforms the parched desert into a fertile oasis of papyrus-lined streams, marshy swamps, cool lagoons, and an amazing array of channels that provide a haven for many different types of plants and animals.

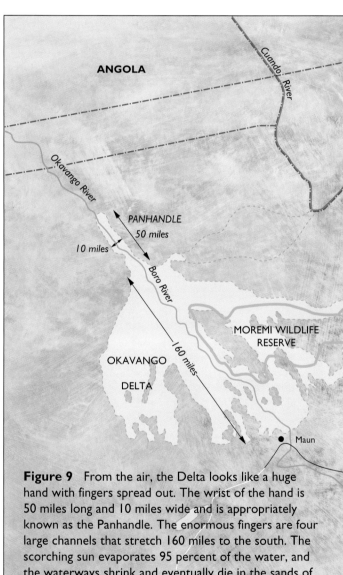

Figure 9 From the air, the Delta looks like a huge hand with fingers spread out. The wrist of the hand is 50 miles long and 10 miles wide and is appropriately known as the Panhandle. The enormous fingers are four large channels that stretch 160 miles to the south. The scorching sun evaporates 95 percent of the water, and the waterways shrink and eventually die in the sands of the Kalahari. A few of the main channels carry water more swiftly through the Delta to the south where it is trapped by a series of faults and rechanneled to the Makgadikgadi Pans, where it evaporates.

Figure 10 (left)   Sometimes storms are accompanied by violent thunder and lightning. In the Kalahari, 50 to 100 people and over 1000 head of livestock are killed by lightning each year.

Figure 11

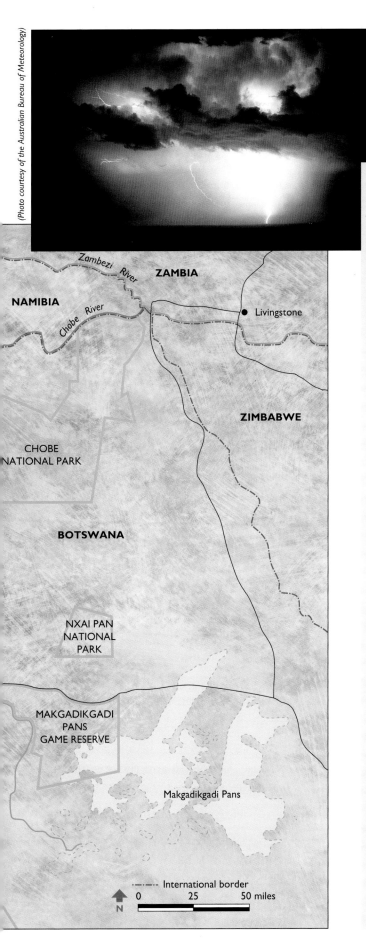

ZAMBEZI River

ZAMBIA

NAMIBIA

Chobe River

• Livingstone

ZIMBABWE

CHOBE
NATIONAL PARK

BOTSWANA

NXAI PAN
NATIONAL
PARK

MAKGADIKGADI
PANS
GAME RESERVE

Makgadikgadi Pans

International border

0   25   50 miles

N

Kalahari rain

The biggest difficulty of living in the Kalahari is the unpredictability of the rains. Only the fittest flora and fauna survive. The wet season may be followed by years of drought. In the scorching heat and cloudless skies, the wind whispers over parched river beds. When the winds die and the clouds begin to darken in November, the thirsty wildlife look to the skies for some relief. The wind and sand whips up violently, and the smell of moistened dust and dampened soil lingers in the air.

Then the storm comes, wreaking havoc with its force. Against the haunting black clouds, sizzling streaks of lightning flash across the sky and huge drops of rain pelt down on the scorched earth of the Kalahari. Then it is no longer a desert, but a green valley full of antelope herds, foxes, lions, jackals, hyenas, springbok, and other creatures lapping up the refreshing rain. In a few days the antelope will be nibbling on new grass, filling their bellies for as long as the feast lasts. The predators will not be far away.

Cooperating to survive

Ecosystems

The plants and animals that inhabit the Kalahari have all had to adapt to the semi-arid environment. The grasses, shrubs, and trees provide shelter, nesting, food, and a source of water for birds, reptiles, mammals, and insects. In turn, these creatures pollinate plants and spread seeds so that vegetation will continue to grow. These plants and animals, and the way in which they depend on each other for survival and regrowth, are together called an ecosystem. If one part of an ecosystem is disturbed, it can affect all the other parts and even lead to the extinction of species.

Above ground, the plant life of the Kalahari must survive the harsh climate. On a hot day the surface temperature can be as high as 160°F, but below the ground it falls at a rate of 18°F for every inch.

Ostriches

The ostrich is the largest flightless bird in the world. A common sight throughout the Kalahari, the ostrich has survived in this dangerous habitat because of its ability to outrun its predators. (It can reach speeds of more than 25 miles per hour.) Its sharp claws and powerful kick are a big help in fighting off attackers.

The tree of life

The huge gray baobab tree with its enormous trunk and bare branches is a familiar sight throughout Africa. In the Kalahari, however, its presence can make the difference between life and death.

Although it is leafless throughout most of the year, the baobab still provides food, medicine, water, clothing, and shelter. When the tree becomes hollow, it holds large amounts of water in its trunk and in reservoirs inside the tree which are fed from rainwater channeled along the branches. The baobab is also known as the "rain tree." It was given this name by early explorers who claimed that when they camped under the tree on fine days, rain actually fell from the branches.

Baobab bark has a high moisture content that satisfies even the "gourmet of bark"—the elephant. People can also make use of the bark by turning it into cords, ropes, nets, and clothes. The baobab's shade can make a big difference, too. Tree-shaded temperatures during the day can be 55°F cooler than in the sun.

Because of drought and the opening up of more land for cattle grazing, the baobabs are starting to decrease in number. This in turn means that the other vegetation and wildlife is also beginning to suffer. Activities such as mining, ranching, and hunting all threaten the fragile ecosystem, and the Kalahari may truly become a barren desert.

Figure 12 (left) Elephants often pull down trees to reach the leaves growing at the top. The damage to this baobab tree is due to the enthusiastic attention of an elephant.

Baobab trees

The enormous baobab tree has been used as a tool shed, dairy, storeroom, bus shelter, and even a prison.

Figure 13 (above) Known as the gourmet of bark, the elephant can be very selective in choosing its diet. Baobab trees are one source that meets with approval.

Figure 14 (left) These meerkats are on the watch for danger. Meerkats, a type of mongoose, have evolved a unique way of dealing with the harsh life of the Kalahari. They live in communal burrows and depend on each other for safety, for food, and for help when needed. They are amongst the most social creatures on Earth.

Food for the desert dwellers

Amazing adaptations

The grasses that grow in the Kalahari sands have evolved special ways of surviving in their unfriendly environment. They have extensive root systems that spread out to trap moisture. Under good grass cover, the moisture trapped deep in the sand after heavy rain may last for many months. Some plants have developed large tubers which store water beneath the sand and nourish the plant. The morama bulb, or gemsbok bean, can grow to 570 pounds and hold 50 gallons of water. As the bulbs have a high protein content, they are also a useful source of food.

Some grass seeds have amazing methods of dispersal and germination. Kalahari plume grass produces feathery white seedheads which are easily blown long distances by the wind. When there is enough moisture, they stick and twist themselves into the sand, so that the seeds, now starting to germinate, can no longer be blown around.

A grappling plant

Grapple-plant is a strange name, but it aptly describes how this plant disperses its seeds. The seed has a trap that locks onto the foot of a passing creature. It may become an important medicinal plant as it has a chemical in its tubers that contains a possible cure for arthritis.

Smaller plants, like the cactuses, have overcome the water problem by retaining moisture in their leaves. Mesembryanthemums and aloes have leaves which hold water for use by the plant itself and for animals and birds that quench their thirst in the height of the dry season. The dry winds carry the ripe seed pods across the sand. Only when it rains will the valves of the pods dissolve and release the seeds so that they may germinate.

Wild species of cucumber and tsama melons encase their seeds in water-filled fruits, which make a nutritious and thirst-quenching meal for many animals. This ensures that the seeds will be carried away and deposited with the animals' droppings to germinate and grow in the next season.

Another Kalahari plant is the truffle, which thrives in the moist underground environment. Very high in fat, protein, fiber, and vitamin B, they make a tasty and nutritious meal for the Bushmen, the indigenous inhabitants of the Kalahari. Truffles resemble potatoes, but are actually a species of fungus. They can only be located by those who have keen eyesight, since the only clue that they exist underground is a series of cracks on the surface.

Figure 17 (right) Trees provide shelter and food for all kinds of creatures, such as this lilac-breasted roller.

(Photo courtesy of Adventure World)

Figure 15 (above) Plants have a tough life under the Kalahari sun, but the rains that come at the end of the year bring a welcome relief and a wealth of new colors to the land as the region's flowers start to bloom.

Edible plants

More than 200 species of edible plants have been found in the Kalahari.

Figure 16 (above) The fruit of the baobab tree, like the nuts and fruits of the acacias and other trees, provides sustenance for the birds, animals, and people of the Kalahari.

Small creatures
of the Kalahari

Ancient insects

Some of the smallest creatures to depend on the Kalahari grasslands are the termites that have lived there for millions of years. Amazingly, fossil termites of 100 million years ago show no differences in body form from the termites of today.

These insects have survived so long because of their ability to adapt to their unusual environment. The nests of the harvester termite are deep in the ground—this way they avoid extremes of temperature and retain moisture. The workers have well-developed eyes (unlike other termite species which are blind), and their heads are protected from the sun's glare by their horny, brown outer covering. In the cool and safety of the hive, the workers process the food by eating it, partly digesting it, then feeding it to others.

Without grasses to feed on, the termites would gradually disappear from the more remote regions of the Kalahari. This would mean hungry grazing animals would starve, since the animals often depend on eating termites in times of drought.

Figure 18 Although they may appear desolate, the sand dunes of the Kalahari provide valuable shelter for many small creatures, from insects and snakes to gerbils and meerkats.

(Photo courtesy of Peter Lemon, Peregrine Adventure)

Thermal dancing

This is a special cooling system used by lizards in the Kalahari. When the ground becomes too hot they stand on alternate pairs of legs, keeping the other two legs raised in the air so that they are cooled.

(Photo courtesy of South African Tourist Board)

Figure 19 (right) While larger creatures find the sand dunes inhospitable, small creatures, such as insects, reptiles, and some small mammals, are right at home. They are able to burrow into the sand to escape the heat, avoid water loss, hide from an enemy, or lie in wait for prey. This ground squirrel is keeping watch at the entrance to its burrow, on the alert for predators.

Under the Kalahari dunes

Beetles, especially ground beetles, are the most common insect group in the Kalahari. They are fierce predators with powerful pincers, and can obtain moisture from the body fluids of their prey and retain it. They hunt by moving quickly on the ground in the coolness of the night. Flatter species of beetles can "swim" through the sand, making them very efficient predators.

Reptiles adapt extremely well to the desert environment. Their reproductive system does not need water and their hard skin retains moisture. Many species of snakes live below ground to escape the intolerable heat of the summer. Blind snakes and worm snakes are primitive species that have short blunt heads and highly polished scales. Their body design allows them to burrow deep into the sand to feed on termites.

Shield-nosed snakes spend the day in rodent burrows and come out at night to hunt when the air is cooler. The deadliest reptile is the burrowing adder, which has the distinct advantage of being able to strike its victim sideways. It preys on lizards and rodents that live in underground passages.

Like snakes, rodents also conserve their water and keep cool by burrowing deep underground and hunting only in the cool of the night. Gerbils supplement a dry diet of seeds

(Photo courtesy of Popperfoto/Sporting Pix)

Figure 20 (above) Termites are very important in the massive food chain that extends throughout the grasslands of the Kalahari. In the winter when the annual grasses die off and provide no nutritional value to other grazing creatures, the termites are still able to thrive on them. The termites themselves become food for other animals during times of scarcity.

with succulent plants. Their droppings create a richer soil in which plants can grow.

In a long drought, even a burrow cannot protect animals from heat and hunger. While larger animals leave the Kalahari to search for food and water, the smaller ones aestivate until the rains come. Aestivation is similar to hibernation. Creatures aestivate, or sleep, until the drought breaks.

Desert antelopes

The gemsbok

Only those creatures that can survive without drinking water stubbornly refuse to be conquered by the cruel desert. One such animal is the ingenious and beautiful gemsbok, which closely resembles the mythical unicorn. It is a powerfully built antelope of the oryx family that has adapted to water conservation better than any other large herbivorous animal.

By panting rapidly, the gemsbok is able to cool the blood flowing to its brain. This means it can survive temperatures of up to 110°F. By allowing its body temperature to rise, it does not need to perspire, and thereby conserves water.

In fact, the gemsbok never needs to drink water. It grazes at night and collects the dew that forms on the leaves of grasses and shrubs, as the cold temperatures reduce the amount of moisture the air can hold. The plants can also soak up this dew, providing a source of water for animals.

The springbok

The springbok is a small antelope, so named because of its habit of leaping into the air. Springboks can endure the desert sun because they are ruminants—that is, they have an extra stomach in which they digest special plant material and store moisture for use in times when water is scarce. These migratory animals have the ability to drink water so salty that it would kill other species.

Figure 21 (above)   As well as the gemsbok, other species of antelopes—springbok (shown here), greater kudu, red hartebeest, and eland—have also been able to adapt to the harsh interior of the Kalahari. Each species has a habitat in which it is able to withstand the conditions, but when droughts are long and dry they have the migratory sense to move off in search of rain and fresh pastures. Less than a century ago, herds of springbok numbering from 50,000 to several million journeyed vast distances across the Kalahari. A single herd can cover an area of 80 square miles on a 13-mile front. Such huge herds trample to death all living things in their path and cause havoc to any farms they cross.

Figure 22 (right)   Water-dependent animals such as zebras and elephants once lived in the grasslands of the central Kalahari, but as the last water pans dried up with the increasing heat, these animals left.

(Photo courtesy of South African Tourist Board)

(Photo courtesy of South African Tourist Board)

(Photo courtesy of South African Tourist Board)

Figure 23 (above lower)   A gemsbok plunges through a crocodile's habitat to the relative safety of the river bank. Large herds of gemsbok still march along the dry waterways of the Auob and Nossob rivers where prides of lions laze under camel-thorn trees waiting for the night hunt.

Threats

The rinderpest disease is a virus that causes fever and loss of appetite and eventually leads to death. It is highly contagious and spreads by direct contact with the infected animal, or through contaminated grasses and water. A rinderpest outbreak in 1896 devastated livestock and wild antelope populations, greatly reducing their numbers.

The loss of large areas of land to farms has also contributed to a decline in the antelope population. Now the herds are scattered across the isolated landscape of the Kalahari.

Predators

A delicate balance

For centuries farmers have killed the large predators of the Kalahari, considering them pests when in fact they play an important role in conserving the grasslands. For example, harvester termites are capable of removing the entire grass cover of an area, which means that grazing animals will starve in times of drought. Termite predators, such as the bat-eared foxes, can consume billions of insects per square mile per year. Where these animals have been exterminated by farmers, there can be a huge increase in termite numbers.

Other persecuted predators are aardvarks and aardwolves, which are able to catch the termites with their large sticky tongues and by using their acute powers of hearing.

Silver foxes

Silver foxes catch most of their prey by scratching out reptiles and rodents from their sand dwellings.

Pythons

A python does not have to eat a daily meal as it is capable of swallowing large animals, such as young impala. The python secretes a large quantity of saliva to lubricate the swallowing process and in this way it can complete eating the unfortunate prey in about an hour.

Night hunters

Most of the Kalahari's predators hunt at night when it is cooler. The foxes do not have to depend on water availability as they extract moisture and minerals from their prey. Lions are the fiercest nocturnal hunters in the Kalahari and yet these large beasts often have to survive on small prey such as rodents, birds, springhares, and bat-eared foxes. When the rains come to the dune woodlands and valleys, they have greater choice, including giraffes, dudu, and gemsboks.

Figure 25 (above)   When farmers kill animals as pests, they end up affecting many more animals than they might imagine. When the numbers of termite predators are diminished, termites flourish and consume vast quantities of grass in direct competition with other grazing animals such as antelopes.

Figure 24   In the dry season, lions have to roam an area of up to 385 square miles and are forced to mix with new prides in foreign areas just to survive.

Figure 26

The brown hyena is an endangered carnivore that has adapted to the harsh Kalahari best of all. It feeds on the kills of other carnivores and uses its strong jaws to break bones. It forages alone at night and is cunning enough to steal from larger predators. A long coat helps it to keep warm in the cold desert nights, especially during the winter.

The use of a large communal den is also important to the survival of the species. When a larger predator, such as a lion, kills one of the mothers, the cubs can still survive as the other mothers share food from hunting. About 70 percent of brown hyena cubs in the central Kalahari are adopted as orphans by other female hyenas. These youngsters will stay together in the nursery until they are mature enough to fend for themselves.

The great migration

When the rains come to the Makgadikgadi Pans, dry lake beds are covered by sheets of water that stretch over hundreds of miles. The crusty mineral salts on the surface of the pans dissolve and the new water brings an abundance of wildlife. Tiny shrimps, crustaceans hatched from eggs buried in the salty mud, come alive—to the delight of winged creatures. Flamingoes in their thousands, pelicans, ducks, and wading birds forage for food and algae. Even the ostrich, which can tolerate extreme heat and live with little water, is excited by the new rain.

Birds thrive in the acacia woodland beyond the Makgadikgadi grasslands. The bushy blackthorn acacias, ideal for secretary birds to nest in, also provide cover for them to stalk and kill poisonous snakes. The hollow of the baobab tree is also used by birds, such as the barn owl to breed in.

As rain falls across the dry land, narrow channels form and begin to drain toward the Makgadikgadi basin. Zebras and wildebeests abandon their usual habitats and follow the rains. The whole landscape is transformed as many large grazing animals and larger predators arrive on the scene. As they trek across the grasslands, they kick up the hot sand with their hooves, causing clouds of dust to rise into the hazy, reddened skies.

Wildebeests

Wildebeests are the most migratory of the Kalahari animals. They are the only large herbivores that have to survive the dry season by feeding on grass. Because of this limited diet, wildebeests are forced to wander in search of better quality grasses. As the water pans and grasses die out, the rain in the distance acts like a magnet. Nobody knows why the wildebeests move north for water and south for food. However, it is possible that they move to the drier south for the minerals found in the Makgadikgadi salt pans.

The migratory herds are not as large today as they used to be, because the routes to water have been blocked by fences and farms. Fences were

Figure 27

(Photo courtesy of Peter Lemon, Peregrine Adventure)

erected to control the spread of the deadly foot-and-mouth disease carried by cattle, to comply with regulations governing the export of meat. The result was tragic. Half of the central Kalahari's large animals perished, unable to reach water. Zebras, elephants, and buffaloes are also affected by fencing. In the last decade they have been forced out of central Kalahari to the north, near the Chobe River.

Figures 28 & 29 (above and left)   The paradise of the rain-filled pans of the Makgadikgadi ends shortly after the last of the rain. The scorching heat quickly dries up the small scattered pans on the grasslands and the water-dependent animals such as zebras, wildebeests, elephants, and buffaloes must return to the permanent lakes and rivers outside the Kalahari Desert. These migratory herds now have to journey greater distances because the Kalahari is becoming more arid.

The delta of plenty

In the 1850s, a Swedish explorer, Karl Andersson, became the first European to have the privilege of watching the extraordinary life-cycle in the Okavango Delta. He wrote of it as a place of "indescribable beauty." This is no surprise, as the waterways and islands of the Delta are an oasis for a variety of plants and animals. On floating beds of papyrus, birds of 400 different species perch, nest, or lie in wait for the ripple which sends them diving into the cool water for their tasty dinner. There are some 65 species of fish in the Delta, including tiger fish with tiny razor-sharp teeth.

Lions, leopards, cheetahs, and elephants can all be found here, but it is the birds of the Delta that benefit most of all. Saddlebill storks, herons, and African skimmers fish the open water, while African fish eagles feast on the catfish and tilapia fish in the waterways. At night the fish are still prey—to the Pel's fishing owl, the only fish-eating owl in Africa.

No one is fooled by the apparent paradise of the Delta. Each spring when the water in the swamps starts drying rapidly, there is an urgent migration as reptiles and fish head for the deeper channels. The rate of evaporation is so fast that many fish and small animals are caught unawares and a massacre begins. Flocks of large birds swoop down for the feast, joined by hungry otters, and the cycle of life and death continues in the Delta.

(Photo courtesy of Peter Lemon, Peregrine Adventure)

Figure 30 (above) In tranquil lagoons, exquisite water-lilies float majestically as frogs and insects perch themselves on the large leaves. In this aquatic wilderness, crocodiles bask in the sun, while the water giants, the hippopotamuses, trample along the narrow Savuti Channel. The hippopotamuses are important residents because they feed on the waterlilies, papyrus, and reeds which would otherwise block the channels between the islands.

Figure 31 (left)
The Delta is a meeting ground for animals of all species—birds, fish, antelopes, elephants, and big cats, such as the cheetah shown here.

Hippos

Hippos spend most of the day partially submerged in water. They move easily along the riverbed on webbed toes. They can also close their nostrils and stay under water for up to five minutes. They have an important role to play in keeping the Delta's waterways open by trampling through the narrow channels during their nightly forage for food.

Figure 33 (right)   It is the birdlife that seems to benefit most from the Okavango Delta paradise.

The Bushmen of the Kalahari

For the last 20,000 years, a remarkable group of hunter-gatherers have lived in parts of southern Africa, using the sun and stars to guide them across the vast plains. These people are called Bushmen, or San, and are the earliest race to have lived in the Kalahari. Until about 3000 years ago, they were the exclusive inhabitants of southern, central, and parts of eastern Africa. The secret of their survival has been their detailed knowledge of the land and their respect for its resources. There are still some Bushmen in the inhospitable Kalahari sandveld (desert), where they hunt and gather food the way their ancestors did.

From AD 500 the San had to share their homeland with a new race of people—the Bantu.

Archeologists cannot agree on where the Bantu originated, but it is believed that they came from west Africa, near Cameroon, and spread through to central and southern Africa. Between 6000 and 12,000 years ago, when the Sahara was not a desert but a savanna with lakes and a variety of wildlife, the Bantu population moved in and lived there. However, when the climate changed around 4000 years ago and the area became a desert, they began to migrate to other parts of Africa.

When the Bantu arrived in the Kalahari region, it is believed that they introduced the Bushmen to iron implements and cattle grazing. At first the two races coexisted in harmony, but as time went on the Bantu's lifestyle, which depended on sheep and cattle, changed their relationship with the hunter-gatherers.

Owning livestock meant wealth and

(Photo courtesy of Graham Romanes, Community Aid Abroad)

Figure 34

The Bushmen

The name Bushmen was given to the people of the Kalahari by early Dutch settlers at the Cape, perhaps because they lived in the bush or used a strong-smelling powder made from particular bushes.

The Tsodilo Hills in the Kalahari contain thousands of ancient paintings depicting the Bushmen's way of life, wild animals, and traditional customs.

Figure 35 (right) A !Kung woman prepares an omelette from an ostrich egg, using a tortoiseshell as a basin.

Figure 36 (below) A Bushmen camp during the summer months. In the background, meat is hanging to dry for storage during the winter.

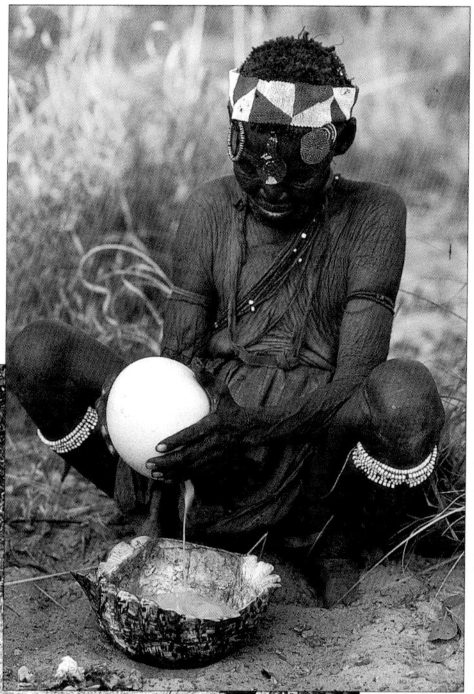

(Photo courtesy of Anthony Bannister)

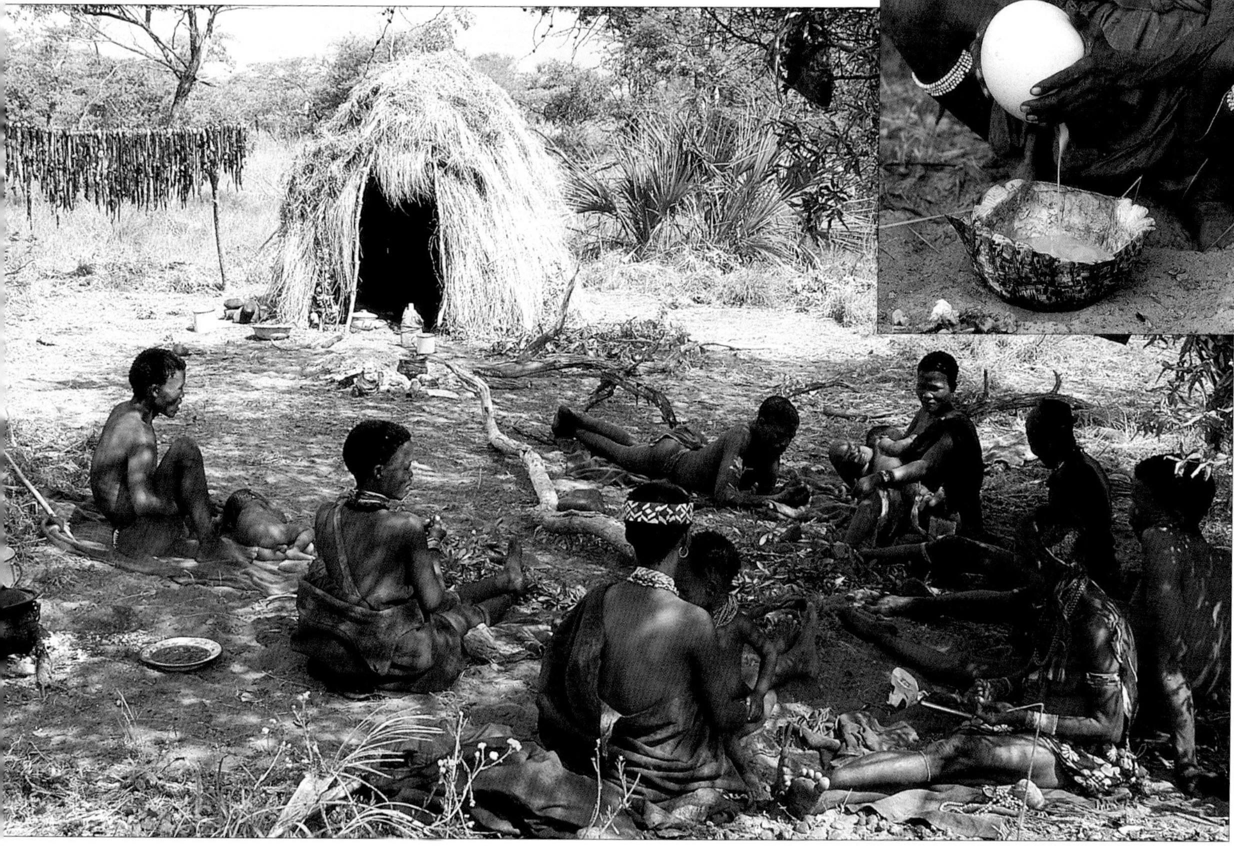

(Photo courtesy of Anthony Bannister)

power. The BaTswana people, who were Bantu pastoralists from the south, became the dominant culture in the region now known as Botswana, and they still are today. The Kgalagari, who were also herders, were not quite as powerful and were employed as farm hands and servants to the rich BaTswana pastoralists.

When it became too difficult for the two cultures of hunter and pastoralist to live in the same region, the San began their trek west into the Kalahari. They continued to move into harsher environments where nobody else would be able to interrupt their way of life ... or so they thought. Then Europeans arrived.

(Photo courtesy of Coo-ee Picture Library)

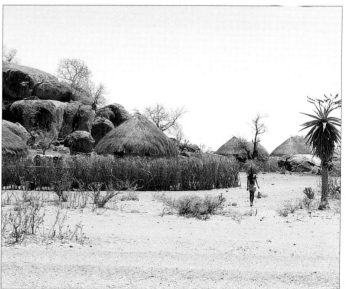

Figure 37 Typical dwellings in a Kalahari community.

Contact with Europeans

The first real contact the Bushmen had with Europeans was when a Dutch explorer, Jan Wintervogel, made an expedition in the north of Cape Province in 1655. Settlers soon started moving inland, and conflicts began to break out. The Bushmen found it easier to kill the grazing sheep and cattle than to travel great distances to hunt wild animals. During this unsettled period in history, hundreds of Bushmen were shot by the settlers and many were taken prisoner.

With more Europeans invading land previously used for hunting and gathering, the various Bushmen groups broke down. Some were absorbed by other indigenous peoples such as the Drakensberg and Cape Bushmen.

The last main group to settle in the northern Kalahari were the Herero. The Herero are descendants of refugees who fled Namibia after a revolution against the German colonists in 1904. During their trek they lost all their cattle and had to start their new life as servants to the rich BaTswana. Slowly they built up their herds and today have regained their status as cattle ranchers and herders.

Today there are around 55,000 Bushmen in the Kalahari region. Most of them live in Botswana, while just over 10,000 are in the bordering countries of Namibia and Angola. That the Bushmen of the Kalahari have survived these invasions is mainly due to two factors—their resourceful skills for surviving in an unfriendly environment and their isolation from other cultures. However, the traditional hunter-gatherer way of life is becoming a thing of the past: less than 2000 San live solely in this manner due to the influences of modern Western lifestyles. It is not the people who face extinction, but their way of life.

Figure 38 (below)   The Herero were the last main group to settle in the Kalahari. Their way of life, which is based on cattle grazing, is quite different to that of the Bushmen, and sometimes brings the two groups into conflict over land.

(Photo courtesy of The African Wildlife Safari Co.)

Figure 39 (above)   European and other settlers have brought their own way of life to the Kalahari. This Kalahari farmhouse, with its stone walls and thatched roof, is in strong contrast with the more open dwellings of the Bushmen.

Figure 40   When Vasco da Gama, a Portuguese navigator, landed on the Cape's west coast in 1497, he described the Bushmen as people with no cattle who gathered plant foods and honey, and hunted antelope. During the following 150 years many Europeans visited the Cape and there was much trading with the Khoi people, who were herders and owned cattle.

Figure 41 (above)   European traders appeared on the scene in the 1800s in search of ivory, ostrich feathers, and animal skins. They came armed with guns to hunt and oxwagons to plunder unknown regions. Widespread killing of game meant that the Bushmen were forced further into the Kalahari, where they remain to this day.

Groups of Bushmen

There are three main groups of Bushmen in southern Africa—the !Kung, the G/wi and the Nharo. They are scattered throughout the Okavango Delta, Angola, and southern Botswana. Within these three main groups are many subgroups that have lived in isolation from one another for so long that they speak completely different dialects and are unable to understand one another.

The Bushmen live and move around in groups of families, which may vary in size from 12 to 50 people. Groups may join together depending on the supply of food available. They place great emphasis on getting along with one another, and choose to share their wealth to emphasize the importance of harmony within the group. Ownership is an unknown word to these gentle people of the wilderness, which may be a reason why they have had no wars, and have continued to live in peace for thousands of years.

Nearly half of the San's food requirements come from hunting, but they kill only for food and not for sport. The males are the hunters, but equally important is the females' task of gathering.

(Photo courtesy of August Sycholt)

Figure 42 (right)   The customs and lifestyle of the Kalahari Bushmen provide an example of living in balance with the environment.

Figure 43

(Photo courtesy of Coo-ee Picture Library)

Poison arrows

Almost all of the Kalahari's Bushmen use the larvae (grubs) of a flea beetle for poison. The larvae bury themselves in small cocoons below the ground. The San dig up these cocoons and carry them around until they are needed. To make a poisonous spear, the cocoons are opened and the grub is removed. The grub is then rolled between thumb and forefinger until it is liquified, the head is nipped off, and the contents are spread on the arrow head. Eight to ten grubs are needed for one arrow.

Bushmen languages

Although there are many different Bushmen languages, all use click sounds which involve movement of the teeth, the tongue, and the lips. The symbols for the various types of clicks are written down as !, /, //, #, 0.

Finding food

Hunting

The biggest challenge to Bushmen hunters is stalking and killing large animals such as antelopes, giraffes, and wildebeests. When the hunter is within a 50-foot range, he fires his arrow, aiming for a fleshy part of the animal where the poisoned arrow tip will quickly take effect.

In !Kung groups, the hunter must always be modest about his kills because hunting is not competitive. Meat, as with all things, is shared equally among the members of the group. If a man has successfully hunted many animals, he is expected to stop for a while to give the rest of the hunters a chance to prove their skills.

The meat doesn't belong to the person who killed the animal, but to the owner of the arrow used. Because the hunters borrow their arrows or accept them from the group, they are all indebted to one another at some time. In this way the group shares its spoils, nobody goes hungry, and there is no need to be envious, as the

Figure 44 Knowing how to store water is just as important as knowing where to find it – empty ostrich shells and hollow baobab trees make excellent water holders.

Figure 45

Tsama melon

A person can live on tsama melon for more than six weeks, as the plant is 90 percent liquid.

Hippo hunters

The baYei tribe were aquatic hunters who would go hippo hunting in their *mekoro* (dugout boats). They would glide quietly into a group of hippos, and plunge a hand-held harpoon with ropes attached into the victim. Then they towed the hippo through the water until the rest of the hunters had a chance to finish the kill with spears. Sometimes the hippo would get its revenge by overturning the boat, and attacking the hunters with its deadly jaws.

wealth is equally distributed. The values of sharing, friendship, and group living have been vital in contributing to the Bushmen's survival.

Gathering

Women are regarded as equals in Bushmen culture. Every day they gather a large amount of food in the form of moisture-bearing plants. This is extremely important to the group because 90 percent of the water the Bushmen consume actually comes from plants. In a dry environment such as the central and southern Kalahari, a water source is essential. In the scorching desert heat, women and children armed with digging sticks and leather bags gather the treasures that lie hidden beneath the sandy dunes. At the end of the day they spread out their harvest for all to share—truffles dug from the earth, succulent tsama melons, handfuls of sun-dried berries, and tasty mongongo nuts and pods, nutritious roots, and moist tubers.

Figure 46

Protected animals

Of the 262 species of animals found in the Kalahari, only 80 are hunted. Some are considered to be too special to be killed. The elephant, for example, is not hunted because the San believe it has the intelligence of a human. Ostriches are too precious to be killed as their eggs provide the San with food, and the egg shells and feathers can be made into ornaments. It also runs too fast to be caught.

Mystic faith

Bushmen believe that there are two supernatural beings who have power over them. N!odima, the creator of the world, is invisible and all powerful, and G//awama, who has less power but can appear in any shape or form, is responsible for disease, misfortune, and wrong doing.

In the constant battle to overcome the evil G//awama, the Bushmen employ their own defense—trance dances. The !Kung people name illnesses after certain animals, and in their dances they call on that animal to help cure the illness. The men go into a trance-like state, dancing and leaping in a circle around a fire as the beat of the women clapping increases in volume and tempo. The sick are believed to be cured by the touch of one fortunate enough to have achieved a trance-like state.

Rock paintings and engravings found in the Tsodilo Hills, north of the Okavango Delta, depict some of these dances. No one knows who painted the images, but the dances are still performed by the !Kung today. For example, the Eland Dance is used to cure ailments of the heart, and the Giraffe Dance is for ailments of the head.

(Photo courtesy of Kagga Kamma Private Game Reserve)

Unlike other traditional African cultures, Bushmen groups have no "medicine man" who has the power to cure the sick. Nor is there a chief or leader. The Bushmen believe: "Each one of us is a chief over him or herself." Partly because of this, the Bushmen don't have much influence in the governing of the countries where they live.

(Photo courtesy of Peter Lemon, Peregrine Adventure)

Figure 47 (left) At night the community gets together around the fire to eat, tell stories, sing, or dance, sometimes until dawn.

Figure 48

The San story of creation

In the beginning the Earth was covered with water. Across the dark waters the legendary San hero, the praying mantis, was carried by a bee. The bee became weary as it searched for dry land on which to lower the mantis. When it saw a great white lily in the darkness, it dropped the mantis and with it the seed of the first human being. In the morning, when the sun's rays warmed the flower, the mantis woke and, from the seed the bee had left, the first San was born.

Some of the paintings in the Tsodilo Hills show a mythical two-horned snake that controls the waterholes, deciding who can drink and who cannot. The snake is said to bleat like a goat, and rise up out of the water with large, shining eyes. Recent sightings of a python in one of the springs in the Tsodilo Hills bear out the Bushmen's belief in this folktale.

Threatened culture

In addition to the Bushmen, the Kalahari is home to many other ethnic groups. The herders include the Nama and Damara, who speak a click language. The Herero, BaTswana, and Kgalagari are mainly involved in herding cattle and goats, but some have farms and ranches or work in other occupations. The Ovambo and Afrikaners (originally from Holland, Germany, and Britain) live mostly by ranching and growing crops. Afrikaners also have businesses in the main towns.

The Bushmen call themselves "red people" to remind other groups that they are different. According to their view, the "black" people are mainly herders who move their livestock from place to place in the traditional African lifestyle. The "white" people are mainly ranchers who fence their land, and deal in the business side of the ranching.

Because the Bushmen have lived in small, scattered groups without a recognized leader and with no concept of ownership, they have not been regarded as citizens with land rights. Therefore, many of them have been deprived of their rightful land and traditional way of life. They now have to compete with wealthy ranchers and experienced herders for their livelihood. The process of change and modernization has brought a better life to only a few Bushmen.

The Bushmen are caught between wanting to keep their traditional culture of hunting-

(Photo courtesy of Anthony Bannister)

gathering and wanting the modern goods and services enjoyed by others around them. Because they cannot afford to own their own herds of animals, much of the Bushmen's time is spent looking after cattle belonging to others in exchange for the bare necessities—clothes, food, and a little money.

The Bushmen in the northern Kalahari

Figure 49 (below) A !Kung woman constructs the frame of a grass hut using flexible poles. Skills such as this are in danger of dying out.

Figure 50 (left) These women in typical Herero dress are actually refugees who have fled from Namibia to Botswana. The Herero are one of the many groups spread throughout the Kalahari.

Figure 51 (left) The Kalahari is home to a wide range of peoples. These children are from one of the many groups involved in cattle herding.

Figure 52 Cattle farms are doing a great deal of damage to the Kalahari – to the land itself through overgrazing, and also to the water supply and all those who rely on it.

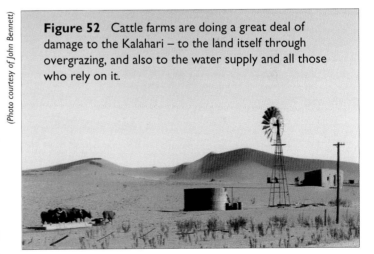

have also been affected by a war which was fought in their region. In the 1970s and 1980s a war between South Africa and a movement called SWAPO (South West Africa People's Organization) disrupted the Namibian Bushmen's way of life. South African soldiers pressured the !Kung to join them in their fight against SWAPO. During this time, the Bushmen gave up hunting and gathering and lived mainly on money paid by the South African army, as well as by looking after livestock. This meant that a generation of children missed out on learning the skills needed to survive in the bush as their ancestors did.

Future of the Bushmen

As boreholes open up large areas of the Kalahari to cattle farmers, the Bushmen are left with less and less land. There are only two areas where the land rights of Bushmen are protected—the Central Kalahari Reserve in Botswana and the Bushmanland in Namibia. Is it fair to force a race who are used to hunting in large tracts of land to live in an enclosed area where the water supply is unreliable and plant foods are scarce?

In good times as many as 3000 San live within the Central Kalahari Reserve, but when times are tough only about 800 remain there.

The old way of life as hunters and gatherers is becoming a thing of the past. While Bushmen children attend school to help them adapt to a new way of life, their culture and traditions are at risk. The Bushmen may be doomed to be absorbed by the other races who live in the Kalahari.

Unlike the Bushmen, whose traditional lifestyle has been hunting-gathering, the other groups rely on cattle for their income. Owning cattle means wealth and status for the herders and ranchers in the Kalahari region, as cattle are

(Photo courtesy of Peter Lemon, Peregrine Adventure)

Figure 53 Many people share the Kalahari – from the villagers adapting to a Western lifestyle to the San who are torn between the new world and their own ancient one.

(Photo courtesy of Anthony Bannister)

one of Botswana's largest exports. The problem is that there are too many cattle crowded into a small area.

As the cattle are driven deeper into the arid lands bordering the Kalahari, more water needs to be found. When this is not available on the surface, boreholes have to be drilled and water extracted from the underground springs. The spread of cattle farther into the interior has had many devastating effects. One of these is the disruption of the migration of wild herds to the northern rivers and lakes (the only sources of water during drought) due to the erection of fences to avoid the spread of foot-and-mouth disease.

More than two million wild animals have died of thirst and starvation since the cattle boom began in Botswana, partly due to the 1800 miles of fences that now cover the country. The Kuke Fence, which divides Botswana in half, prevents large animals from reaching the northern waterways.

Figure 54 (above)   A !Kung hunter instructs his children how to use a bow accurately. The Bushmen are among the world's last surviving hunters.

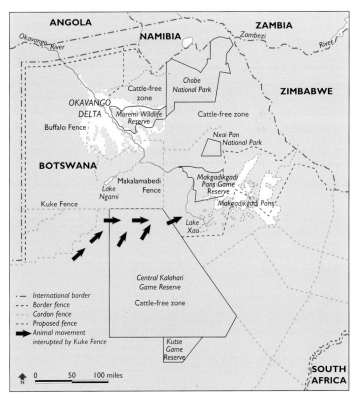

Figure 55   More than 1800 miles of fences now cover Botswana, including the Kuke Fence which divides the country in half.

The value of land

Overgrazing in the Kalahari is a serious environmental problem. It contributes to the destruction of grasslands in a region where valuable plants are already threatened by drought. Cattle also compete with native animals for land and food. Until the 1980s, more than 60 percent of people in west Botswana depended on hunting for their livelihood. Now they must travel many days to find animals to hunt. As a result, many people now depend on drought-relief aid.

Reserves and conservation

Have authorities learned from past mistakes? It seems that with the growth of the cattle industry, the Botswana Government decided it was time to take quick action. Under the Fauna Conservation Act of 1963, it began to set aside large areas as sanctuaries. Today 17 percent of the total land area has been set aside as national parks and reserves.

Commercial hunting (hunting wild animals for profit) also threatens the fragile balance of wildlife in the Kalahari. Much of Botswana is divided into controlled hunting areas with no more than six hunters operating in a designated area in one week. Hunting licenses and fines mean that wildlife has some form of protection from unscrupulous hunters. The Wildlife Department has been established to alert the government to serious decreases in the numbers of animal species and to discover ways to provide protection.

The problem of overgrazing and the expansion of cattle ranching is still unsolved. Cattle herds managed in the traditional method are allowed to roam freely on land owned by the group. The Kalahari grasslands are excellent for grazing, but the vegetation is very fragile and, unlike the more fertile lands, it takes longer to recover. Overgrazing could easily turn the grasslands into a dust bowl.

The National Land Management and Livestock Project funded by the World Bank aims to overcome the problem of overgrazing and bad livestock management in communal grazing areas. New slaughterhouses are being built, and better education programs in farming methods are being introduced.

Figure 56 Can native wildlife compete with cattle when cattle have always been associated with wealth and status? Perhaps as the world's wild animals continue to be threatened with extinction, the Kalahari's native animals will be fully appreciated and protected.

(Photo courtesy of The African Wildlife Safari Co.)

(Photo courtesy of Adventure World)

Figure 58

Figure 57 (above) Tourists are also a potential hazard to the environment. Tourism has become the fourth largest income earner in Botswana after diamonds, cattle, and copper. The government has wisely recognized the value of wildlife and developed the Wildlife Conservation Policy, which separates tourist areas and hunting areas into zones. People are encouraged to farm native animals to maintain their numbers.

(Photo courtesy of The African Wildlife Safari Co.)

Endangering the rhino

Rhinoceros horn is regarded as valuable in Asian countries for its mystical power. A rhino can yield between 11 and 22 pounds of horn, earning poachers more than $35,000. As a result, the rhino is fast disappearing from the Kalahari region. The last white rhino was shot in 1890 in the northern Kalahari and the last black rhino in 1936 near the Okavango Delta. The Botswana Game Department reintroduced rhinos to the Moremi Game Reserve, but their current population is unknown.

Figure 59 (above) The steady decline of wildlife worried the traditional hunters, so the BaTswana people living on the eastern edge of the Okavango Delta formed a wildlife reserve on their land, where animals could be protected from professional hunters. This became known as the Moremi Wildlife Reserve—the first wildlife sanctuary in southern Africa created by indigenous African people on their own land.

Threatened waterways

Diamonds

The Orapa diamond mine in the dry Kalahari saltpans causes great concern for environmentalists. To extract diamonds from the ground requires huge quantities of water, which may eventually be taken from underground waterholes or from the Delta. Water is the most valuable asset in the Kalahari, and the removal of any amount from the Delta could cause irreversible damage to the ecosystem.

(Photo courtesy of Adventure World)

Figure 60 Besides the threat that cattle herding poses to the traditional hunting lands, there is also mining. In some parts of Botswana and Namibia, diamond miners have drained away water supplies and made the land unsuitable for either cattle or wildlife, let alone human beings.

The tsetse fly

The Okavango Delta is also under threat from the decline of the tsetse fly. The fly provided a very effective way of keeping people and cattle away from the northern waterways. When blood-sucking tsetse flies bite humans or animals, they transmit disease-carrying parasites. Wild animals are naturally immune to the disease, but humans are not.

When a disease known as rinderpest broke out in the early 1900s, up to 90 percent of the wild game were wiped out in some areas. More than a million animals were slaughtered over the next 40 years in an effort to stop the disease. Deprived of food, the tsetse fly began to move north, so people were free to settle on the edges of the Delta. But as time went on, the fly returned to wage war. It took many years of trial and error, but finally the insecticides DDT and dieldrin were successful in destroying the fly. Unfortunately dieldrin has also been responsible for killing 69 species of birds, reptiles, and fish.

The tsetse fly has now virtually disappeared from the Delta. People and livestock are

Guardian of life or death?

The tsetse fly transmits a disease called sleeping sickness in humans and *nagana* in animals. This sickness affects the central nervous system and, if untreated, can cause death.

safe from the deadly disease. However, the absence of the fly that had guarded the Delta since its formation could create an environmental disaster if cattle, people, or greedy governments should misuse the area. Fortunately for now, the Okavango is recognized as a World Heritage Site. Its conservation is of great importance to the World Wildlife Fund and the Botswana Government, which aims to protect and conserve the incredible ecosystem.

A deadly disease

Rinderpest is a highly contagious viral disease that affects cattle and game with symptoms of fever, restlessness, and loss of appetite. At the end of the 1800s when the disease swept Africa, it killed tens of millions of animals. A vaccine was found by scientist Dr Robert Koch, and the disease was eliminated.

Figure 61 (above)   The Okavango Delta, an oasis of lush vegetation and animal life on the edge of the central Kalahari sands, is now classified as a World Heritage Site. This should prevent the spread of towns and industry into the area, which could potentially do a large amount of damage to a fragile ecosystem.

Figure 62 (above)   Among the many tragedies of our world ranks the death of over a million of the unique animals of the Kalahari, brought about in a deliberate attempt to deprive the disease-carrying tsetse fly of its food source.

A new harmony

Africa has been known as the "Dark Continent" because early Europeans considered it a place of mystery and danger. However, it was a lack of understanding that created the danger to new settlers, and prevented them from living in harmony with the environment.

The indigenous peoples, on the other hand, lived in harmony with this continent. Until the end of the 1800s, the Bushmen culture and the environment of the Kalahari remained intact.

The Bushmen's ancestors enjoyed a land that provided equally for all its inhabitants. Today, this ancient and vast region is threatened by human interference. Will the Kalahari survive the modern age? The solution may lie somewhere in the Bushmen's culture which has remained unchanged for 20,000 years, together with worldwide awareness and the full cooperation of the Botswana Government.

Figure 63 All too often the problems faced by growing civilizations have been caused by the lack of understanding of their environment and the way animals exist side by side in an ongoing cycle of life and death.

(Photo courtesy of South African Tourist Board)

Glossary

aestivation   A state similar to hibernation in which animals go into an extended "sleep" to survive long periods without water.

anthropologist   Someone who studies the lifestyles of people of the world.

archaeologist   Someone who studies the lifestyles of people who have lived in the past, through the things they have left behind.

arid   Dry; having no regular rainfall. A large portion of the Kalahari is arid or semi-arid.

band   A community of between ten and a hundred hunter-gatherers who live together as nomads.

borehole   A deep well that brings underground water to the surface by the use of pumps.

bush   A wild area of land. Bushveld is a low-level area in southern Africa covered with scrub.

Bushmen   The common name for the hunter-gatherers of southern Africa; they were the first inhabitants of the Kalahari.

carnivores   Meat-eaters.

clicks   Sounds used in many southern African languages.

colony   A country separated from, but subject to, government by another country.

drought   An extended period of time during which there is little or no rain.

ecosystem   The interconnected web of plant and animal life that survives in a particular environment.

game   Wild animals hunted for food or sport.

habitat   The area in which an animal or plant naturally lives.

herding   Keeping and moving livestock (such as cattle) from place to place.

hunter-gatherers   People, like the Bushmen, who live by hunting and gathering food rather than farming.

indigenous   Original inhabitants of a particular area.

livestock   Animals kept on farms to produce food and other needs, including cattle, sheep, and goats, which provide meat, milk, and wool or leather.

migration   The movement of people, animals, or birds at a certain time of year to a new habitat.

nomadic   Moving from one place to another, usually in search of food.

overgrazing   Grazing more cattle than an area can support. In overgrazed areas the vegetation has no chance to regrow, and the area can become barren.

pans   Natural depressions in the ground containing water, mud, or salt.

pastoralism   A way of life based around the herding of domestic animals, such as cows or goats.

resources   Things that people take for their own use from the environment, such as plants, animals, water, or minerals.

San   A name for the Bushmen.

succulents   Fleshy or juicy plants, such as a cactus.

sandveld   Desert.

savanna   Open grasslands.

trance   A dream-like state.

Index

THE COMPOSITE GUIDE

IN THIS SERIES

Auto Racing

Baseball

Basketball

Football

Golf

Hockey

Lacrosse

Soccer

Tennis

Track and Field

Wrestling

THE COMPOSITE GUIDE

to **BASEBALL**

NORMAN L. MACHT

CHELSEA HOUSE PUBLISHERS
Philadelphia

Produced by Choptank Syndicate, Inc.

Editor and Picture Researcher: Norman L. Macht
Production Coordinator and Editorial Assistant: Mary E. Hull
Design and Production: Lisa Hochstein
Cover Illustrator: Cliff Spohn

Cover Deisgn: Keith Trego
Cover Art Direction: Sara Davis
© 1998 by Chelsea House Publishers,
a division of Main Line Book Co.
Printed and bound in the United States of America.

1 3 5 7 9 8 6 4 2

Library of Congress Cataloging-in-Publication Data

Macht, Norman L. (Norman Lee), 1929-
      The composite guide to baseball / Norman L. Macht.
         p. cm.— (The composite guide)
      Includes bibliographical references (p.) and index.
      Summary: Traces the story of baseball from its beginnings to its
   first great stars, notable players of today, and speculation about
   its future.
      ISBN 0-7910-4723-7
      1. Baseball—United States—History—Juvenile literature.
      2. Baseball players—United States—Juvenile literature.
   [1. Baseball. I. Title. II. Series.
   GV863.A1M33 1997
   796.357— dc21   97-30934
                                                                    CIP
                                                                     AC

CONTENTS

THE *SHOT* HEARD ROUND THE WORLD

For more than 150 years baseball has provided exciting, suspenseful, and memorable events for its fans. Teams battle almost every day for six months to reach the ultimate goal: the gold and glory of a World Series victory.

Sometimes, after thousands of pitches have been thrown, the long, grueling pennant race is decided by one pitch, one split-second of action that separates the winners and losers.

Way back in 1904, a pitcher named Jack Chesbro won 41 games for the New York Highlanders, as the Yankees were then called. But on the last day of the season he threw a wild pitch that scored the winning run in a game that made Boston the pennant winner instead of New York.

On October 14, 1960, in the deciding game of the World Series in Pittsburgh, the lead seesawed back and forth between the Pirates and Yankees. After eight innings, the Pirates led, 9–7. But the Yankees fought back and tied it in the top of the ninth. Then Pittsburgh second baseman Bill Mazeroski led off the last of the ninth and hit a home run to win the championship. Pittsburgh fans are still celebrating to this day.

One swing of Toronto outfielder Joe Carter's bat ended the 1993 World Series. Down 6–5 to the Philadelphia Phillies in the last of the ninth of Game 6, Carter hit a three-run home run that made the Blue Jays the champions on the last pitch of the year.

A forlorn Jackie Robinson (42) watches as the New York Giants celebrate their stunning come-from-behind victory in the 1951 National League playoff. Dodgers pitcher Ralph Branca, who gave up the game-winning home run to Bobby Thomson, starts the long, sad walk to the center field clubhouse.

But baseball does not reserve all its dramatic climaxes for the World Series. Perhaps its most famous "shot heard round the world" capped what many who watched it called a miracle. On August 12, 1951, the Brooklyn Dodgers enjoyed a $13\frac{1}{2}$-game lead over the New York Giants. The Dodgers were the best team in the National League; from 1946 through 1956 they would win six pennants, losing three others on the last day of the season. The confident Dodgers taunted their hated crosstown rivals, the Giants. This made the Giants fighting mad; they won 16 in a row and cut the Dodgers' lead to 6 games. They stayed hot, getting the half-inch breaks that often make the difference between winning and losing. With only one week to go, Brooklyn still led by three games. Then, in what seemed to many fans to be one miracle win after another, the Giants caught up with them. The teams were tied with one game to play.

Every baseball fan in the country sat glued to a radio on that Sunday, September 30. The Giants won their game in Boston while the Phillies were leading the Dodgers, 8–5. It looked as if the Giants' miracle comeback had succeeded. But the Dodgers staged their own thrilling comeback, winning the game thanks to a spectacular catch by Jackie Robinson, then a 14th-inning home run by Robinson.

The Giants and Dodgers finished in a tie for first place, forcing a three-game playoff for the pennant. They split the first two games, and when the Dodgers took a 4–1 lead into the last of the ninth of the showdown at the Polo Grounds, it seemed that the Giants were finished and the better team would win. With their ace, Don Newcombe, pitching, Brooklyn fans were on the edge of their seats, ready to celebrate as soon as the last out was made.

Then things happened. An infield hit, a single, a double, and suddenly the score was 4–2 and two men were on base with one out. Bobby Thomson, the Giants third baseman, faced relief pitcher Ralph Branca. Thomson swung at the second pitch. The ball arced into the left field seats and into history. The Giants' 5–4 victory touched off a delirious celebration that became frightening in its wild frenzy, while Dodgers fans sat stunned in disbelief.

Fans far away from New York had been equally caught up in the dramatic climax to the miraculous season. One told a Chicago newspaper, "I've seen a lot, but this is just the greatest. Years from now, when we tell our grandchildren about this, you know what they'll do? They'll sneer and walk away and say that we're nuts. They'll never know how these guys have reached deep inside us and grabbed our hearts with both hands."

The many games played during each long season offer thousands of chances for a spectacular or record-breaking performance, always unpredictable. On May 1, 1920, two pitchers pitched an entire 26-inning game that ended in a 2–2 tie, the longest game on record. On May 2, 1917, fans in Chicago saw both the Cubs and Reds pitchers throw nine-inning no-hitters against each other. One day in June 1938 a young Cincinnati lefthander named Johnny Vander Meer pitched a no-hitter in Boston. Not too unusual, but four days later in Brooklyn he pitched another one. Nobody else had ever thrown two no-hitters in a row.

The Yankee Stadium scoreboard shows all zeroes for the Brooklyn Dodgers as New York pitcher Don Larsen pitches to second baseman Jim Gilliam in the seventh inning. No Brooklyn batter reached base in the only perfect game in World Series history, October 8, 1956.

In the 1956 World Series, Don Larsen of the Yankees pitched a perfect game, setting down all 27 Brooklyn batters he faced. The 64,519 who were at Yankee Stadium and the millions more watching it on television saw something that had never happened in a World Series.

Baseball continues to captivate the millions of people who play it or watch it, with its excitement, its stories, and its heroes. After seeing thousands of games during his 60 years as a player, manager and executive in baseball, Branch Rickey was asked, "Aren't you tired of watching baseball?"

"No," Rickey replied. "The next game I see may be the greatest one of all."

THE AMERICAN NATIONAL GAME OF BASE BALL.

GRAND MATCH FOR THE CHAMPIONSHIP AT THE ELYSIAN FIELDS, HOBOKEN, N.J.

2 HOW BASEBALL BEGAN

Nobody actually invented baseball. It just grew out of games people played, as far back as the first caveman who picked up a rock and hit it with a tree limb. The earliest written account of anyone playing catch occurred at least 3,000 years ago in Greece. In the sixth century, St. Augustine admitted to playing ball instead of studying on a warm summer day.

Emigrants from England brought a game called "cat ball" to America in the early 1700s. Boys and girls played various kinds of ball games on village greens, using rules that varied from one colony to another. Some of the games used bases and some did not. In one version, called "town ball," there was no limit to the number of players on each team. A baserunner was tagged out by throwing the ball at him. If it hit him, he was out. Nobody wore a glove or a catcher's mask.

When young gentlemen gathered for social occasions, they sometimes chose up sides and played a leisurely game. A club in New York City called the Knickerbockers organized a ball team in 1845 at the suggestion of a 25-year-old bank clerk, Alexander Cartwright. He and his friends set about improving the game and writing down the rules. They divided the field into fair and foul territory, and fixed the distance between the bases at 30 paces. (Men's paces varied in length, so not every diamond was the same. In 1857 they settled on 90 feet.) Baserunners were put

An early game of base-ball is played at the Elysian Fields, a cricket pitch in Hoboken, New Jersey, where many historians say the first game between the Knickerbockers and another team under the "modern" rules took place in 1846.

out by tagging them with the ball or throwing the ball to a baseman instead of aiming it at the runner. Later they set the number of players at nine on a side.

These changes formed the foundation of the modern game of baseball. Other innovations followed: 9 innings for a game; pitchers throwing underhand from 45 feet, and later 50 feet; batters declaring whether they wished the ball thrown to them high or low. In the beginning, a base on balls required 9 called balls; it took 45 years for it to gradually evolve down to the present 4, and for 3 strikes to mean "You're out."

In 1884 pitchers began throwing overhand, still only 50 feet from home plate. Now that pitchers were throwing the ball harder, catchers began to wear a mask and chest protector. A few of them wore a thin buckskin glove with the fingers cut off to protect their hands,

An old book illustrates various bat and ball games played in England in the 18th century.

Bat and Ball.

sometimes slipping a slice of beefsteak under it. They took a lot of teasing from other players who continued to play barehanded.

In 1893 the pitcher's box was replaced by a rubber slab and the pitcher moved back to 60 feet 6 inches. Since 1900, when home plate was changed from a 12-inch square to its present five-sided, 17-inch width, baseball's playing rules have changed very little. If Napoleon Lajoie, who batted .422 in the American League's first season in 1901, came back today, he could step into the lineup without having to look at the rule book.

Settlers from England had also brought with them their own national game, cricket. Baseball did not evolve from cricket, although there are a few similar terms used in both games. At the time the Knickerbockers were laying out the diamond for their "New York ball," cricket was the national game in America. Philadelphia was the center of cricket activity, but there were teams in cities and universities in the east and midwest. A team from England toured the United States in 1859 and played before large crowds.

Cricket is a slow-paced game that takes several days to complete, and the faster game of baseball rapidly gained favor among working men and gentlemen's clubs. Brooklyn was an early hotbed of baseball activity.

The Knickerbockers' brand of baseball spread north to Boston and south to New Orleans. Colleges, businesses, working men, and social clubs formed teams. They were all amateurs, playing the game because it was fun and a healthy form of exercise for men who worked from dawn to dark six days a week. Teams of carpenters challenged boilermakers,

Alexander Cartwright, a member of the 1845 Knickerbockers, introduced baseball to mountain men and Indians on his way west to look for gold in 1849. Later he went to Hawaii, where he taught the natives the game.

fishmongers challenged clerks. Every town big enough to put nine men and boys on the field had a team. Rivalries between neighboring towns quickly heated up, the games becoming the highlight of many a Fourth of July holiday. Games between rival cities, like New York and Brooklyn, drew crowds of 10,000 and more, who sat in carriages or on the ground around the open, unfenced playing fields.

Henry Chadwick, an English-born cricket writer for the *New York Times*, fell in love with baseball. He began to write about the games in the newspaper, and soon other papers covered the matches. The publicity gave the game a big boost. Chadwick invented the first system for keeping score, and created the box score to enable his readers to know who did what in the games. For his role in making baseball popular and better understood by its new fans, Chadwick is known as the "Father of Baseball."

Americans have always had a penchant for organizing and joining clubs. In 1858 representatives of 25 baseball teams met and formed the National Association of Baseball Players. They considered changes in the rules, and scheduled games against each other. Two years later the association had grown to 70 teams.

Wearing straw hats and fancy flannel uniforms, teams began to travel hundreds of miles, enjoying the hospitality of their host clubs along the way. The games inspired friendly wagers between players and teams; the large, enthusiastic crowds who turned out included gamblers who would bet on every play, even every pitch. Newspapers gave banner headlines to the events, which were often the social highlights of the summer.

The Civil War spread baseball, as many soldiers saw the game for the first time. Here Union prisoners of war play in a southern prison camp in Salisbury, North Carolina in 1863.

Then came the Civil War in 1862, which stopped the growth of organized baseball as millions of young men switched to blue or gray military uniforms and rifles instead of bats. But the fierce fighting did not stop the spread of the game. It was played in army camps on both sides, and sometimes between enemy regiments during a lull in the battles. Many of the soldiers who came from farms and small towns had never seen baseball. They took the game back home with them after the war ended in 1865. As a result, two years later the National Association convention attracted representatives from 237 clubs.

Until that time, baseball had remained almost purely an amateur pastime. One young fastball pitcher, Jimmy Creighton, was suspected of being paid to pitch for the Brooklyn Excelsiors in 1859. In 1863 Al Reach, a British-born cricket star, became the first openly professional player when he signed for $25 a week with the Philadelphia Athletics.

Two things made it inevitable that baseball would become a business. Rivalries between towns grew so intense, citizens clamored for their civic leaders to field winning teams, even if they had to hire a star player to wear the home uniform. And the game had become so popular, businessmen and investors decided there must be a way to make a profit from it.

FIRST NINE OF THE

CINCINNATI

(RED STOCKINGS) BASE BALL CLUB.

THE MAJOR LEAGUES

In 1869 a group of Cincinnati businessmen got together with one purpose in mind. They wanted a winning team to represent their city, even if they had to pay all the players. They got what they paid for.

They hired a cricket star, Harry Wright, to be the manager. Wright went out and signed the best players, including his brother, George, for a total payroll of $9,500. The red stockings the team wore gave them their name.

The Cincinnati Red Stockings toured the nation, winning all 57 games they played—except for one tie—against local teams. They disbanded after one more year, but professional baseball was here to stay. Players organized their own teams, formed a nine-team league, and scheduled games against each other. But it didn't last. Many teams did not play out their schedules. Players jumped from one team to another during the season. Chaos reigned.

The owner of a Chicago team, William A. Hulbert, got disgusted and started his own league, called the National, in 1876. He was determined to enforce the rules to keep the game as honest and stable as possible. The league banned beer sales in the stands, and no games were played on Sundays. It was not an instant success. Some teams lost money and quit. Players gambled on games almost as much as the spectators did. Fans preferred to watch their

The 1869 Cincinnati Red Stockings, the first all-professional team, were undefeated in their first season.

friends play on town teams rather than watch the professionals.

By 1879 the *Cincinnati Gazette* declared, "The baseball mania has run its course. It has no future as a professional endeavor."

That was not the last time baseball's demise would be prematurely predicted. New stars came along and captured the public's attention. Club owners built new grandstands and set aside special days for ladies to attend free. Attendance picked up and teams became more profitable.

When the National League expelled the Cincinnati Reds for selling beer and playing on Sundays, the Reds started a rival major league called the American Association. They found seven other teams to join them and signed away some National League stars. The baseball war continued for a few years, after which the two leagues cooperated. They agreed to play a postseason series between the league champions, thus creating the first version of a World Series.

Everybody was now making money from the baseball business except the players. The two leagues had made an agreement that set a salary cap of $2,000 per player. Injured players were not paid while they were out of action. They had to pay for their uniforms. The players got fed up with this arrangement and in 1890 formed their own league, just as they had done in 1871.

Now there were three major leagues competing for the fans' limited attention and attendance. Nobody won that war. The Players' League folded after one season; a year later the weakened American Association went out of business. Only the stronger National League survived, expanding to 12 teams.

Meanwhile teams in smaller cities and towns were organizing into minor leagues. As professional baseball expanded there was less control over it. Once again the game suffered from gambling scandals. The National League had a monopoly on major league baseball. Its club owners were allowed to own interests in more than one team; they fought among themselves for control of the league. Players fought with umpires, some of whom swung back with fists and masks. Hooligans hurled bottles and other missiles at players and umpires from the stands. Umpires sometimes picked up the bottles and threw them back at the customers.

The riots and roughnecks on and off the field drove away respectable patrons, and the experts proclaimed, "Baseball as a commercial enterprise is a dead business."

The Boston Red Sox won the first modern World Series in 1903. The overflow crowds in Boston ringed the field, creating hazards for outfielders. There was no World Series in 1904, then it became an annual event until the players' strike in 1994.

As often happens, where most people saw chaos and decline, someone else saw opportunity. Ban Johnson, a former baseball writer from Cincinnati, was the president of the Western League, a minor league in the midwest. He believed that baseball had a future, but only if the umpires were respected, the players were honest, and the ballparks were clean, safe, pleasant places to spend an afternoon.

Johnson renamed his league the American. When the National dropped four of its 12 teams in 1901, he moved into those vacated cities and declared his league a major league. His agents lured National League stars by doubling and tripling their salaries, and another baseball war began. This one lasted for two years, ending with a peace treaty in January 1903. That year

Children of immigrant families quickly took to baseball. Here they play stickball in a tenement alley in Boston in 1909.

the American League moved out of Baltimore and into New York, and the Yankees were born. For the next 50 years there were no changes in the eight-team lineups of the two leagues.

Baseball boomed. Men and women played the game on farm fields and city streets, in prisons and army camps, in the ocean and indoors. The millions of immigrants pouring into the New World from Europe quickly realized that the best way to fit in with Americans was to become a baseball fan. New modern grandstands of steel and concrete replaced rickety, inflammable wooden bleachers. Beginning in 1905, the World Series became the biggest sports event of the year, enthralling the nation for a week or more every October.

As a new and exciting form of entertainment, baseball's popularity soared on the wings of its early stars, and the game had a sky full of them.

Every army and navy base fielded many teams. Here sailors on the battleship USS Washington in 1911 pose beside one of the ship's big guns.

THE KING
AND THE BABE

Baseball's early stars came in all sizes and shapes. There was 5' 4" Wee Willie Keeler, who wielded a magic bat that "hit 'em where they ain't," placing the ball just out of the reach of fielders with uncanny skill; stout, bow-legged Honus Wagner, who scooped up ground balls and dirt with his huge hands and led the National League in batting eight times and in stolen bases five times, despite his crooked legs and barrel chest; and Big Ed Delahanty, a 6' 1" slugger, one of five brothers who played in the major leagues in the 1890s.

But a few early stars shone above all the rest. Twenty years before Babe Ruth was born, Michael Joseph "King" Kelly was baseball's first national hero in the 1880s. The big, black-haired Irishman was rarely seen alone. Wherever he went, his face decorated with a shiny handlebar mustache, his stylish clothes studded with brilliant diamonds, Kelly attracted a parade of admiring boys and adoring young ladies. When King Kelly entered a dining room or saloon, he brought a generous spirit and a good time for all with him.

Kelly was also a smart, fleet-footed, creative ballplayer, first with Chicago's National League champions, then with the Boston Beaneaters. He was mainly a catcher and outfielder, but he played every position at some time and led the league twice in batting. Kelly was most celebrated

Michael "King" Kelly became baseball's first national hero in the 1880s, through songs and newspaper stories before there was radio, television, or movies.

as a daring baserunner. At that time only one umpire worked a game. Behind the ump's back, Kelly often dashed straight from first base to third without going near second. If he was on second base and the umpire had his eye on a ball hit to the outfield, Kelly would dash home without visiting the neighborhood around third base. His spectacular slides inspired a popular song, "Slide, Kelly, Slide."

One day Kelly was on the Boston bench during a game. A pop foul was hit near the bench. Kelly saw that the Boston catcher could not reach it, so while the ball was still in the air he jumped up, yelled, "Kelly now catching for Boston," and caught the ball barehanded. Later the league changed the rules so the umpire had to announce replacements.

At the height of his popularity, after batting .388 and leading the Chicago Colts to the 1886 pennant, Kelly was sold to Boston for $10,000, then an astounding sum for a ballplayer. Feeling betrayed, the stunned Chicago rooters boycotted the Colts, while Boston's heavily Irish population cheered the King's arrival.

Kelly didn't help the Beaneaters win, but his popularity never waned. In the winter he appeared in vaudeville acts, and was on his way to play the Palace Theater in Boston when he died of pneumonia at the age of 36.

In the 1890s and early 1900s baseball players were considered by the public to be little better than hoodlums. Few had much schooling. They gambled, drank, and brawled on and off the field. They subjected umpires to verbal and physical abuse, kicking, pummeling, and spraying them with tobacco juice. First class hotels would not let a baseball team in the door. The players slept two to a bed in cheap rooming houses.

Then in 1901 Christy Mathewson, a tall, handsome, clean-living, college-educated pitcher became a star for the New York Giants. It was said of Matty that he pitched as much with his brain as his arm. He was a crackerjack chess and checkers player who could defeat several opponents at the same time while playing blindfolded.

Matty won his first eight starts, four of them shutouts, and quickly became a national idol as well as a New York favorite. Three years in a row he won 30 or more games. In the 1905 World Series he pitched three shutouts in six days.

A college star with a reputation for clean living and good sportsmanship, Christy Mathewson was idolized by fans while winning a National League record 373 games between 1901 and 1916.

A calm, dignified gentleman who would not pitch on Sundays and never argued with umpires, the 6-foot, blue-eyed Mathewson boosted baseball's image on his broad shoulders. He epitomized all that was considered the best of America. One teammate said of him, "He looked like he meant well toward the whole world." And the whole world reciprocated. Known by the nickname "Big 6," Matty was so famous that a letter with nothing on the envelope but a big "6" was once delivered to him 3,000 miles away in California. More than any other player, he made baseball respectable for the whole family.

As his victories mounted to a National League record 373 over 16 years, Mathewson's fans and admirers cheered his successes, and they mourned more than he did when he suffered some heartbreaking World Series losses toward the end of his career.

His lungs damaged by poison gas while in the army during World War I, Matty never fully recovered. Cynical sportswriters in the press box wept openly when they learned that he had died just before the first game of the 1925 World Series.

In contrast to Mathewson, nobody ever cried for the terrible-tempered Tyrus Cobb, not even the few ballplayers who showed up for his funeral. No player was ever hated or hooted or booed more than Ty Cobb, but nobody ever played the game more ferociously or effectively. If they wanted to boo him, the fans had to come out to the ballpark, so his Detroit Tigers drew big crowds wherever they played. The fans who hated him also grudgingly admitted that they came out to see him because he was the best ballplayer many of them would ever see.

Born in Georgia into a family of Confederate Army veterans, Cobb fought his own civil war with teammates, opponents, fans, and everybody else he came in contact with, as well as his own personal demons.

Beginning in 1905, Cobb played 24 years, all but the last two with Detroit, forging the highest career batting average in the books at .367. He declared that the basepaths belonged to him, and he slid into and cut up and knocked over anybody who got in his way. He handled a bat like a magic wand, and once on base he loudly challenged catchers to try to throw him out. Cobb's total hits and stolen base records were eventually topped, but Ty Cobb blazed a trail no player has ever been able to follow. In his own cantankerous way, he gave fans their money's worth of thrills and plenty to talk about through the dead days of winter until the next opening day.

Ty Cobb had to be the best in everything he did, so nobody made him madder than the only person who could overshadow him in the 1920s—Babe Ruth.

Two men are credited with saving baseball at that time: Judge Kenesaw Mountain Landis and Babe Ruth. Baseball fans were shocked when it became evident in 1920 that gamblers had bribed some players on the Chicago White Sox to deliberately lose the 1919 World Series to the Cincinnati Reds. It seemed as if the game's hard-earned reputation for honesty would be destroyed, setting baseball back to its disreputable days of a mere 20 years earlier.

Ty Cobb was the fiercest, fightingest, most competitive player in history. Using his bat, his brain, and his speed, he terrorized pitchers and infielders for 24 years.

Nervous club owners turned to Landis, a federal judge, to restore public confidence. They named him Commissioner of Baseball and gave him unlimited power to do whatever he thought was best for the game. Landis began by banning eight White Sox players from baseball for life. He ruled the game for 25 years until he died in 1944.

George Herman "Babe" Ruth was the best left-handed pitcher in the American League. He had helped pitch the Boston Red Sox to the world championship in 1916 and 1918, winning two games in the 1918 World Series. But Ruth could also hit, and in 1919 he began to play in the outfield when he wasn't pitching.

Of course, to say that Babe Ruth could hit is like saying that birds can fly. He was a natural hitter. In 1919 pitchers were still allowed to cut and scuff the ball, rub it in mud, and spray it with tobacco juice. (Those practices were banned in 1920.) That year Ruth startled baseball fans by belting 29 home runs. The rest of the Red Sox team hit a total of four.

After the 1919 season the New York Yankees bought Ruth, to the anguished howls of Boston fans (78 years later the Red Sox still had never won another World Series because of the "Curse of the Bambino"). As an outfielder in 1920, Ruth stood the baseball world on its ear by hitting 54 home runs, more than any other American League *team*. He hit them higher and farther than anybody had ever seen a ball travel, inspiring the word Ruthian to describe mighty blasts of the future. He also batted .376 and made the fans forget about the game's 1919 scandal. The next year he hit 59 home runs while batting .378.

Before he became famous as a slugger, Babe Ruth was the best left-handed pitcher in the American League. He won three World Series games for the Boston Red Sox.

By the time he topped his own record by hitting 60 in 1927, Babe Ruth was not only the most famous ballplayer in the world, he was one of the most famous people in the world. He was also the most popular.

The phrase "larger than life" aptly describes the Babe. Everybody loved him. Generous to a fault, always out for a good time, happiest when surrounded by kids, equally loved and admired by other players, the Babe ruled the baseball stage until he retired in 1935. He hit the first home run in Yankee Stadium when it opened in 1923 and won the first All-Star Game in 1933 with a homer. He became the highest paid player of his time, lifting the salary levels for all players who followed him. By demonstrating that swinging for the fences was where the big money was, Ruth changed the way the game was played, from the slap-hitting, base-stealing, low-scoring style exemplified by Ty Cobb, who hated him for it.

Other players whose talents helped to swell the game's popularity included Walter Johnson, a tall, long-armed pitcher for the Washington Senators who threw so hard batters complained that they couldn't hit what they couldn't see. Toiling mostly for losing teams, the quiet, widely respected Johnson won 416 games and led the American League 12 times in strikeouts.

The game's greatest right-handed hitter, Rogers Hornsby, had a personality like sandpaper, but fans turned out to watch him hit. Over a five-year period beginning in 1921, he averaged .402, reaching a peak of .424 in 1924.

Jimmie Foxx was called the "right-handed Babe Ruth." The strongest man in baseball, the farm boy from Sudlersville, Maryland, smashed 58 home runs in 1932 and hit 30 or more a record 12 consecutive years.

In its early years baseball was generously populated with eccentric and colorful characters who became fan favorites with their flamboyant antics on and off the field. Many of them were known more by their descriptive nicknames than by their real names: Peanuts and Pepper, Pee Wee and Pretzels, Lefty and Whitey and Bobo and Hippo, and a dozen or more Babes.

And Dizzy. The biggest crowd pleaser and showman of the 1930s was Dizzy Dean, a right-handed pitcher for the St. Louis Cardinals. Diz won more games and laughs than anybody until his career was cut short by an injury in 1937. He grew up picking cotton in Arkansas, but he was smarter than he let on. After his playing days, he mangled the language so much as a game broadcaster that teachers complained about his influence on their students.

On the field, Diz strutted and boasted about how good he was, but he said it wasn't bragging if you could back it up. And he did. Before a game he would tell hitters how he was going to pitch to them, then stand on the mound and laugh after he struck them out. In 1934 he predicted that he and his brother Paul would win 45 games for the Cardinals. They won 49. The next year they won 47.

There were managers like John McGraw, who led the New York Giants for 30 years. McGraw feuded and fought with umpires and every other team in the league while winning 10 pennants. His New York fans loved him; in other cities they threw rocks and deceased produce at his players as they rode to and from ballparks.

Connie Mack, who wore a suit and tie in the dugout, managed the Philadelphia Athletics for 50 years. The tall, dignified Mr. Mack was the opposite of John McGraw, but won nine pennants.

Casey Stengel managed teams that were so bad they were jokes, and Casey was the chief clown. He spun yarns and played pranks and demonstrated the hook slide in hotel lobbies and double-talked and entertained writers and fans of all ages. Later, when he managed the New York Yankees and had the horses, Stengel became a genius, winning 10 pennants in 12 years.

These were some of the people who helped baseball's roots grow deep in the hearts of Americans, making baseball the National Pastime.

5 THE GAME'S NEW ERA

When the Japanese bombed the American naval base at Pearl Harbor, Hawaii, on December 7, 1941, and the United States entered World War II, life in America changed for everyone. Millions of men joined the armed forces. Men and women went to work in factories making the weapons of war 24 hours a day. Blackouts went into effect in cities on the east and west coasts.

Asked if major league baseball should shut down, President Roosevelt said no; the game was important to the morale and relaxation of American servicemen and workers. With hundreds of players in the service, teams relied on oldtimers and teenagers to fill out their rosters. Many minor leagues did suspend operations.

The end of the war in 1945 sparked a booming economy. New homes went up to house returning servicemen and their families. The first new automobiles in four years rolled off assembly lines. And Americans wanted fun. They went to baseball games in record numbers in cities like Cleveland, where Bill Veeck, the game's greatest promoter, fielded a pennant-winning team that drew a league record 2.6 million fans. Thirteen of the 16 major league teams set attendance records in the late 1940s. Night games, a novelty since their debut in 1935, gradually began to dominate the schedule. Returning players, eager to resume their careers, enabled 59 minor leagues to thrive. The Brooklyn Dodgers, run by Branch

Red Barber interviews Dodgers manager Leo Durocher at Ebbets Field in Brooklyn before the first telecast of a major league game on August 26, 1939.

Jackie Robinson played the 1946 season with the Brooklyn Dodgers' Montreal farm team before becoming in 1947 the first black player in the major leagues since the 19th century.

Rickey, who developed the modern farm system, had enough players to field 29 teams.

The three or four years lost during the war virtually ended many players' careers. But some stars, like Cleveland's fireballing right-hander Bob Feller, came back in Hall of Fame style. Feller, while still a 17-year-old high school senior, had struck out 15 batters in his major league debut in 1936. He won 25 games in 1941, then joined the navy. In 1946 he won 26, striking out a record 348.

Far-reaching changes swept baseball in the postwar years. In 1946 Branch Rickey signed Jackie Robinson, the first black player in Organized Baseball since the 19th century, for the

Dodgers' Montreal farm team. Blacks had been limited to playing on teams in their own leagues. In April 1947 Robinson joined the Dodgers and integrated major league baseball. A few months later the Cleveland Indians signed Larry Doby, the first black player in the American League. Overcoming threats, spikings, and constant racial harassment, Robinson led the Dodgers to the 1947 pennant and was named Rookie of the Year. Doby and legendary Negro Leagues pitcher Satchel Paige helped the Indians win in 1948. Baseball led the nation in the march toward equal rights, integrating before many of the nation's schools, hotels, restaurants, and theaters, and the U. S. military.

Few people noticed on August 26, 1939, when Cincinnati Reds third baseman Bill Werber stepped into the batter's box at Ebbets Field in Brooklyn to lead off the first inning. As announcer Red Barber spoke his name, a lone camera behind Barber sent a flickering picture of Werber to a handful of tiny television sets. The experiment was the first televised game. It would be another 10 years before every team showed some of its games on TV.

Gradually the players began to gain more rights from the owners. Under the reserve system, players belonged to the team that first signed them forever. They could be traded at any time; their only alternative to moving was to quit. They had to accept whatever salary the club offered, or stay home. No player could become a free agent unless his team released him.

One man, Curt Flood, objected to being traded and sued to gain the freedom to sign with any team. He lost, but in 1975 players won the right to limited free agency. Salary arbitration made millionaires of average players. By the end of the 20th century the Players Association had gained control of the game.

The most important change in the playing rules occurred in 1973 when the American League introduced the designated hitter (DH). Seeking to boost run production, the league allowed a team to take the pitcher out of the batting order and replace him with a better hitter. The National League rejected the DH, and the two major leagues agreed to play under different rules.

The eight-team National and American Leagues had remained the same for 50 years. There were three teams in the New York area. Chicago, Boston, St. Louis, and Philadelphia had teams in both leagues. St. Louis was the westernmost city; Washington was as far south as they went.

That lineup changed in 1953 when the Boston Braves moved to Milwaukee. The next year the St. Louis Browns were sold to a

Many club owners feared that allowing fans to watch the games free at home would ruin baseball. Eventually, the money from television financed the players' generous pension plan and multi-million dollar salaries. In this picture, two cameras peer over the announcer's shoulders at a 1945 game in New York's Polo Grounds.

Baltimore group, and in 1955 the Philadelphia Athletics became the Kansas City A's, eventually winding up in Oakland.

Once set in motion, baseball's wanderlust rolled on. Not since the 1890s had baseball's map undergone so many changes. The most stunning move came in 1958 when the New York Giants and Brooklyn Dodgers deserted their fans, the Giants moving to San Francisco and the Dodgers to Los Angeles. When the Washington Senators moved to Minnesota in 1961, the nation's capital was without a team and the country's biggest city, New York, had no National League team.

Branch Rickey threatened to start a third major league and move into the vacated cities. Club owners responded to the challenge by putting new teams in New York—the Mets—and Washington, and adding teams in Los Angeles—the Angels—and Houston for the 1961 season. From then until the end of the century, expansion ballooned the original 16 teams to 30, divided into three divisions in each league.

Baseball was now played almost entirely at night, in indoor ballparks and on concrete-hard artificial surfaces in some cities. Players, represented by agents, were free to sign with the highest bidder after a few years in the big leagues. Top salaries surged past $10 million a year. The only thing that remained unchanged from 100 years earlier was the action between the white lines. The pitchers still had to throw the ball, the hitters hit it, and the fielders catch it. Babe Ruth would find the batting helmets (introduced in 1960), batting gloves, and enlarged fielders' gloves unfamiliar, but he could step into the lineup with no problem. Nobody could imagine what kind of salary he would command today.

JOLTIN' JOE AND OTHER SUPERSTARS

Every generation produces players who rise above the rest and live on in the memories of those who saw them. In addition to raw athletic talent, these stars share a pride in what they do and a dedication to excel. They do not rely on luck, but make their own by being mentally and physically prepared for whatever challenges confront them.

The following brief sketches describe some of the greatest players in the game between 1940 and 1980.

Joe DiMaggio was the son of an immigrant Italian fisherman in San Francisco. As a boy, Joe didn't care much for baseball, even though he was the best player among his friends. But he liked working on his father's fishing boat even less. So when his older brother Vince offered to take him to a tryout with the San Francisco Seals of the Pacific Coast League, Joe agreed to go. The Seals signed him.

The New York Yankees bought his contract in 1935 and DiMaggio became baseball's greatest all-around player. He did everything well. He had a classic swing with no wasted motion, a strong and accurate arm, baserunning skills, and unerring baseball smarts. He made no mistakes on the field. "The Yankee Clipper," as he was nicknamed, seemed to glide gracefully across the grass in the vast center field of Yankee Stadium without effort, hauling in fly

Ted Williams (left) and Joe DiMaggio talk hitting before the 1949 All-Star Game. The rival superstars had great respect for each other. Williams, who called DiMaggio the greatest player he ever saw, was himself considered the best hitter in the game.

balls with ease. Three times the Most Valuable Player, DiMaggio inspired his teammates with his pride and professionalism, leading them to nine world championships in 13 years.

Of all his statistics, one unique measure stands out in describing DiMaggio: he hit 361 home runs and struck out only 369 times. No other slugger came close to that ratio. By contrast, Babe Ruth struck out more than twice as often as he connected for a home run.

Joe DiMaggio became a legend in 1941 when he captivated the nation in June and July by hitting safely in 56 consecutive games. The shy, quiet hero became celebrated in a song, "Joltin' Joe DiMaggio," and remained an American idol even when he was in his 80s.

DiMaggio shared the national spotlight in 1941 with Ted Williams, an outfielder for the Boston Red Sox. Williams grew up in San Diego, California with one ambition: to be the greatest hitter who ever lived. And he achieved his dream.

Hitting was his passion. No matter how good he was, he never stopped working at it— studying, practicing, asking questions of pitchers and other hitters, shaving his bats for a perfect grip.

The left-handed hitting Williams had the misfortune to reach his highest batting average in 1941, the same year that Joe DiMaggio's 56-game hitting streak captured all the headlines. Williams batted .406; for more than half a century, he remained the last player to top .400.

Despite losing nearly five years of playing time in two stints of military service, Williams hit 521 home runs and finished with a career batting average of .344, the fourth highest in the 20th century.

Williams never acted like a star or a celebrity. An avid fisherman, he preferred the company of fishing buddies, cab drivers, firemen, and anybody with whom he could talk hitting.

There was another player who starred in 1941 but is largely forgotten today. Pistol Pete Reiser may have become the greatest player who ever wore spikes. At the age of 22, the Brooklyn Dodgers rookie led the National League with a .343 batting average. Fast as lightning, he stole home seven times in one season. But he was too daring for his own good. Eleven times he charged into walls chasing fly balls and had to be carried off the field. His injuries cut short his career, but many of his Brooklyn teammates considered Reiser the greatest player in Dodgers history.

Ted Williams, "The Splendid Splinter," worked to become the best hitter the game ever saw. His keen eyesight enabled him to see the stitches on the pitch coming toward him and to swing only at strikes.

One mark of a champion is being consistent, producing the same numbers year after year. Nobody was ever more reliable than Stan "The Man" Musial. In 21 seasons with the St. Louis Cardinals, the outfielder–first baseman batted .310 or better 17 times. Musial rarely went into a slump. He hit as well on the road as at home and led the league in batting seven times. For two decades Musial was the most difficult puzzle for pitchers to solve, although his batting stance was one no coach would teach. His body was so twisted and crouched, he looked like a man trying to peek around the corner of a building.

Musial was popular with fans in every city in the league, even though he often single-handedly destroyed the home team.

Another champion of consistency was Henry Aaron. A calm, unemotional player, Aaron never hit as many as 50 home runs in a season, but for 20 years he hit between 20 and 47. As he closed in on Babe Ruth's career home run record of 714, Aaron drew death threats and hate mail from people who resented a black player's surpassing one of the popular Babe's long-standing records. Aaron retired in 1976 with a record 755 home runs. His hitting overshadowed his excellent defensive play in left field.

During the 1950s, New York fans had the privilege of watching three future Hall of Fame center fielders in action: Willie Mays of the Giants, Mickey Mantle of the Yankees, and Duke Snider of the Dodgers.

Writers dubbed Mays the "Say Hey Kid" because he often greeted other players with a high-pitched, enthusiastic "Say Hey." They also called him one of the best all-around players of all time. Mays could run, throw, hit, hit for power, and routinely make unbelievable catches. He led the league in home runs and stolen bases, and he is one of only two players ever to rack up more than 20 doubles, triples, home runs, and stolen bases in the same season (1957).

Born in Birmingham, Alabama, Mays began playing in the Negro Leagues, the only professional teams where blacks could play before the Dodgers signed Jackie Robinson in 1946. Mays was 20 when he arrived in New York, and enjoyed playing stickball with kids in the streets of New York as much as the big league game. New York fans were heartbroken when the Giants moved to San Francisco in 1958 and took their beloved Say Hey Kid with them.

Mickey Mantle played for the New York Yankees, but he was a national hero. Mantle overcame many obstacles to become a superstar. A bone disease that began when he was playing high school football in Commerce, Oklahoma, together with numerous leg injuries, forced him to play in severe pain for much of his career. After only one year as a minor league shortstop, he was asked to play the outfield when he joined the Yankees at 19. Mantle had to live up to the heavy publicity and predictions of greatness made by the media. And in 1952 he had to replace the Yankees' leader, Joe DiMaggio, who retired.

Mantle's pure athletic ability overcame all those barriers. He became the greatest switch-hitter in history. Books have been written about his legendary tape measure home runs. Like

In the 1950s and '60s Mickey Mantle became the latest in a line of New York stars who were national heroes, following Joe DiMaggio, Babe Ruth, and Christy Mathewson.

DiMaggio, Mickey Mantle's popularity continued to grow after his playing days ended.

Duke Snider never gained the national stature of Mays or Mantle, but during four seasons in the mid-1950s he hit more home runs and drove in more runs than either of them. Defensively, the pride of Brooklyn was their equal.

Home run sluggers get the loudest cheers, but the fans of this era also witnessed some of the game's greatest pitchers. The most intimidating of them was Bob Gibson. Batters quaked when the 6' 1" right-hander scowled down at them from the mound, leaving no doubt that he considered them the enemy. He did not hesitate to brush them back with a fastball under the chin, and once threw at a batter who was waiting in the on-deck circle.

In 1968 Gibson was so dominating, the rules makers lowered the pitching mound to give hitters a better chance. That year 13 of his 22 wins were shutouts; he allowed only 1.12 earned runs per game. In 17 years with the St. Louis Cardinals, the Omaha, Nebraska native became the second pitcher to chalk up 3,000 strikeouts. In three World Series he won seven consecutive games. Gibson was also a good hitter, clouting 24 home runs and two more in World Series play. He helped himself with the glove, winning nine Gold Glove Awards.

Jim Palmer was not yet 21 when he pitched a shutout for the Baltimore Orioles in the 1966 World Series. Then the 6' 3" right-hander missed most of the next two seasons with arm and shoulder problems that might have ended his career. But he came back to pitch a no-hitter in 1969 and win 16 games against 4 losses.

The last of the high-kicking windup pitchers, Palmer lasted long enough to become the first to win World Series games in three decades, and the first to win three Cy Young Awards in the American League. During his 19 years with the Orioles, Palmer had eight 20-win seasons.

Fifty years after Christy Mathewson retired, New York fans had another handsome, intelligent right-handed pitcher to idolize—Tom Seaver. This time their hero wore a Mets uniform. A hard-working perfectionist, Seaver won 25 percent of all the Mets' victories between 1967 and 1977. Tom Terrific won three Cy Young Awards and struck out 200 or more batters for 10 seasons. Seaver became the 17th 300-game winner.

Lefty Steve Carlton threw the hardest, nastiest slider any batter ever coped with, and he won four Cy Young Awards with it between 1965 and 1988. Tenacious in working on his strength and physical fitness, Carlton concentrated so intently while pitching, he blocked out everything around him. No teammates dared talk to him when he was on the mound. In 1972 he won 27 games, almost half the total victories of his last-place team, the Philadelphia Phillies.

Carlton retired in 1988 with 329 wins and more than 4,000 strikeouts. Only one lefthander ever won more games. That southpaw was Warren Spahn. Despite missing four years while in the army, the stylish, smooth-working Spahn won 363 games in 20 years with the Boston/Milwaukee Braves (the Braves moved to Milwaukee in 1953). Spahn topped 20 wins 13 times. When his fastball began to slow, he became a master at changing speeds and keeping batters off balance. Every pitch he threw had a specific purpose behind it. Spahn was also a good hitter. He hit 35 home runs, more than any other National League pitcher.

Of all the great pitchers of that era, Sandy Koufax came the closest to being absolutely unhittable over a five-year span. But it wasn't always that way for the slender left-hander. Born in Brooklyn, Koufax signed with the hometown Dodgers at 19 and never pitched in the minor leagues. He threw a blazing fastball, but he was wild. It took him seven years to master control of his speed; the Dodgers were then in Los Angeles.

During five seasons beginning in 1962, Koufax pitched four no-hitters, threw 11 shutouts in 1963, set a strikeout record of 382 in 1965, won 111 games against 34 losses,

In the 1970 World Series, Brooks Robinson's dazzling fielding, .429 batting average and two home runs earned him the Series MVP Award. He was the American League's starting third baseman for 15 straight All-Star Games.

and averaged under two earned runs per game. He led the National League in every important pitching department, won three Cy Young Awards, then retired at 31 when the pain from arthritis in his valuable left elbow became too much too bear.

Brooks Robinson was one of the few players fans came out to see because of his fielding. In his 22 years as the Baltimore Orioles third baseman beginning in 1955, the "Human Vacuum Cleaner" made spectacular plays seem routine. He won 16 Gold Gloves and set records that remained far beyond the reach of other third basemen. Robinson was a Hall of Famer as player and a kind, generous, easily approachable All-Star.

These superstars and others left records for future players to aim for and memories that never faded for the fans who saw them.

7 THE RECORD SETTERS

Babe Ruth set many batting records, some of which were later broken. But Ruth never fretted about someone else doing better than he did. "Records were made to be broken," he said.

Statistics and records make up more of the lore of baseball than of any other sport. Some of the game's individual and team achievements are likely to be surpassed by future stars, while others may never be topped. Babe Ruth's 60 home runs in 1927 stood for 34 years until Roger Maris, an outstanding outfielder for the New York Yankees, had one magical year and hit 61. But Maris did not enjoy his year in the spotlight. The ghost of Babe Ruth haunted him throughout the season; the quiet Maris was not a popular choice to dethrone the beloved Babe. The tension as he neared the record caused Maris's hair to fall out in clumps. The record caused a controversy because the baseball season was eight games longer in 1961 than it had been in Ruth's time, giving Maris that many more chances to break the record.

Modern sluggers like Ken Griffey Jr., Frank Thomas, and Albert Belle threaten to make any home run record obsolete in the coming years, including Henry Aaron's 755 career homers.

Another record that may fall to speed demons like Kenny Lofton is Rickey Henderson's 130 stolen bases, set in 1982. Then with the Oakland A's, the fleet-footed Henderson was the

Despite playing the demanding position of shortstop, Cal Ripken Jr. broke a record for endurance that was considered beyond the reach of modern players when he played in his 2,131st consecutive game on September 6, 1995.

Rickey Henderson kept pitchers jittery whenever he got on base, and that was almost half the time he batted.

most productive leadoff batter in history. A single or base on balls almost always became a double. He could hit more than 20 home runs while stealing 80 or more bases every year. Henderson was the first to ring up 1,000 steals.

The hardest man for pitchers to strike out was Joe Sewell, a shortstop for the Cleveland Indians and New York Yankees. In 14 seasons beginning in 1920, Sewell struck out 74 times while batting .312. During one remarkable four-year period, Sewell fanned only four times in 2,000 times at bat, a record that is almost impossible to beat.

Many baseball veterans consider Joe DiMaggio's 56-game hitting streak the toughest record of all to break. Unlike season-long records that enable a player to have some bad days along the way, DiMaggio's feat required at least one base hit in every game for almost two months. That takes a combination of good health, some luck, and staying calm—almost without nerves—as the pressure mounts and the media crush grows day by day.

But who can say what is impossible? Surveys in the past always ranked Lou Gehrig's record of playing in 2,130 consecutive games as the least likely to ever be matched. The star first baseman of the Yankees played through numerous broken bones in his hands, backaches, and fevers from 1925 through 1939. For the next half century nobody came close to threatening his mark. Yet that incredible record fell to Cal Ripken Jr. on September 6, 1995, and the Baltimore Orioles infielder continued to extend his record into the 1997 season.

In Gehrig's time there was no television, and games were not even broadcast on the radio in New York. He had passed the old record of 1,307 games with little notice in 1933, adding to it quietly until a fatal illness forced him to quit on May 2, 1939. The modern media hordes hounded Ripken throughout the 1995 season. He held a press conference in every city where the Orioles played, answering the same questions time after time, and had to stay at a hotel apart from the rest of the team under an assumed name to escape the pressure. Shortstop is a demanding position, yet the strong, 6' 4" Ripken avoided serious injuries and overcame minor hurts that might have sidelined another player, while playing hard at all times.

Ripken's record for home runs by a shortstop may be beaten, but his consecutive game streak will probably survive as long as baseball is played.

Changes in the strategy of the game and the shorter careers of most pitchers compared

The baseball record least likely to fall is Cy Young's 511 wins. The right-hander won more than 30 games five times between 1891 and 1902.

to the oldtimers put many pitching records out of reach. The increased use of relief pitchers and larger pitching staffs make it all but impossible for anyone to win 511 games, as Cy Young did. Walter Johnson's 416 wins is a distant second. Young, a farmboy from Ohio, averaged almost 50 starts a year for 20 years beginning in 1891, and he completed almost 85 percent of them. He pitched more complete games each year than any pitcher *started* in the 1990s. Young spent half his career in the old National League and the rest in the new American League, and was equally successful in both. He also lost more games—315—than anybody.

One modern pitcher did set a record, and he did it by sticking to a relentless conditioning program that enabled him to pitch for 26 years until he was 46. When right-hander Nolan Ryan retired from the Texas Rangers in 1993, he held 53 major league records, including 383 strikeouts in 1973 and 5,714 total strike-outs. A future pitcher would have to average 300 strikeouts a year for 19 years to match him. (John Smoltz led the National League with 276 in 1996.) Six times Ryan fanned more than 300 in a season. He threw seven no-hitters, the last when he was 44. He also walked the most batters—2,795.

Grover Alexander, who shares the National League record of 373 wins with Christy Mathewson, threw a record 16 shutouts in 1916 for the Philadelphia Phillies.

Jack Chesbro won 41 games for the New York Highlanders in 1904; 48 of his starts were complete games. Ed Walsh of the White Sox won 40 in 1908. (Modern pitchers rarely start more than 35 games a year.) In 1904 the Boston Red Sox pitchers threw 148 complete games, a record that is sure to last another 100 years.

The 1906 Chicago Cubs won 116 games and lost just 32. They won the pennant by 20 games, the first of four in five years. Despite longer schedules that began in 1961, no other team has won more than 111 (Cleveland Indians in 1954).

Some records fall every year, but it takes a super performance to challenge the most honored marks of baseball.

8 BASEBALL'S FUTURE

In the winter of 1888–1889, two American baseball teams traveled around the world to promote baseball. They played games in Australia, Egypt, and Europe, but failed to impress their hosts. Except for Japan, where baseball interest began early in colleges before professional teams were organized, baseball remained an American pastime.

One hundred years later, all that had changed. American oil and mining companies had introduced the game to Central and South America. It took root and thrived in Cuba, Mexico, the Dominican Republic, Puerto Rico, and Venezuela. By the 1990s, baseball leagues were expanding in Australia and Europe, except in Britain where it had never overcome cricket. The Anaheim Angels even signed three Russian players, who later became scouts for them in Russia.

Television was largely responsible for the international growth of baseball. The Baltimore Orioles received almost 1,000 requests for media credentials from Japan, England, France, Germany, Czechoslavakia, and Central and South America to witness Cal Ripken's breaking of Lou Gehrig's consecutive game streak on September 6, 1995.

In 1997 major league baseball telecasts reached five continents and almost 200 countries. Major league opening day rosters included 147 foreign-born players from 17 countries. More than one-third of them came from the Dominican

Ken Griffey Jr. was baseball's most popular star of the 1990s. Griffey believed that playing ball should be fun, and nobody enjoyed the game more than he did.

Republic, where teams had set up clinics and local leagues that produced a rich harvest of players, especially outstanding infielders. Not one of the Los Angeles Dodgers' five starting pitchers spoke English as his native language.

In 1996 the San Diego Padres and New York Mets played a regular season series in Monterey, Mexico. The next year the Padres and St. Louis Cardinals traveled to Hawaii for a series. Major League Baseball looked forward to expanding beyond North America, and a truly worldwide World Series came closer to reality.

Other changes in baseball's major league structure were in the wind. For the first time, the 1997 season included interleague play. Each American League team played four or five National League teams, with the games counting in the standings. Continued expansion into new cities—Phoenix, Arizona, and Tampa, Florida, being added in 1998—increased the likelihood of an extensive realignment of the two traditional leagues. The separate identities of the National and American Leagues, with their separate umpiring staffs and league records, seemed destined to disappear.

The effects of change cannot always be predicted. Disagreements between players and club owners over changes in the game had led to several walkouts by the players in the 1980s and 1990s. The longest occurred in 1994, forcing cancellation of the World Series for the first time in 90 years, and a delayed start of the 1995 season. Despite a labor agreement reached in 1995, many problems were left unresolved. As the baseball business became bigger and salaries continued to rise, the possibility of future walkouts remained.

Hideo Nomo, a Japanese pitcher for the Los Angeles Dodgers, was one of almost 150 foreign-born players in the major leagues in the 1990s.

One aspect of baseball did not change: the action on the field, which is the basis of the lifelong passion for the game held by baseball fans. New superstars appeared. Dominating pitchers such as Greg Maddux and Randy Johnson, and hitters capable of record-breaking performances like Tony Gwynn, Gary Sheffield, Mark McGwire, Barry Bonds, Ken Griffey Jr., Frank Thomas, and Kenny Lofton, provided heroes for another new generation of fans.

With an expanding world of talent to draw from, and millions of American youngsters playing in leagues for all age levels, baseball was rapidly becoming an International Pastime with an unlimited future as the 21st century arrived.

Tomorrow's superstars are playing somewhere today on sandlots and Little League diamonds all over the world.

CHRONOLOGY

1845   The New York Knickerbockers design a baseball diamond that results in bases 90 feet apart.

1858   Amateur players organize the National Association to schedule games and standardize rules.

1869   The Cincinnati Red Stockings field the first all-professional team.

1876   William A. Hulbert organizes the National League.

1901   Ban Johnson creates the American League.

1903   The first modern World Series is played, the Boston Red Sox defeating the Pittsburgh Pirates.

1914   A rival major league, the Federal League, is organized, and lasts two years.

1920   Federal Judge Kenesaw Mountain Landis is named baseball's first commissioner.

1933   The first All-Star Game is played, the American League winning, 4-2, in Chicago's Comiskey Park.

1935   The first night game is played in the major leagues in Cincinnati.

1938   The first baseball game is televised, Cincinnati at Brooklyn.

1939   The National Baseball Hall of Fame opens in Cooperstown, N.Y.

1953   The Boston Braves move to Milwaukee.

1958   The Brooklyn Dodgers move to Los Angeles and the New York Giants to San Francisco.

1961   Baseball expands for the first time when the American League adds teams in Minnesota and Los Angeles.

1969   The major leagues form east and west divisions, inaugurating pre-World Series playoffs.

1973   The American League adopts the designated hitter rule.

1980   Nolan Ryan becomes the first million-dollar player.

1981   A player strike stops major league games for six weeks.

1994   A player strike cancels the World Series for the first time in 90 years.

MAJOR RECORDS

INDIVIDUAL RECORDS

BATTING

Season

Batting Average: Hugh Duffy, 1894 – .438

Hits: George Sisler, 1920 – 257

Home Runs: Roger Maris, 1961 – 61

Runs Batted In: Hack Wilson, 1930 – 190

Stolen Bases: Rickey Henderson, 1982 – 130

Bases on Balls: Babe Ruth, 1923 – 170

Lifetime

Batting Average: Ty Cobb, – .367

Hits: Pete Rose – 4,256

Home Runs: Henry Aaron – 755

Runs Batted In: Henry Aaron – 2,297

Stolen Bases: Rickey Henderson – 1,186
  (through 1996)

Strikeouts: Reggie Jackson – 2,597

PITCHING

Season

Wins: Jack Chesbro, 1904 – 41

Strikeouts: Nolan Ryan, 1973 – 383

Complete Games: Amos Rusie, 1893 – 50

Earned Run Average: Dutch Leonard, 1914 – 1.01

Winning Pct.: Roy Face, 1959 – .947 (18-1)

Shutouts: Grover Alexander, 1916 – 16

Innings Pitched: Amos Rusie, 1893 – 482

Lifetime

Wins: Cy Young – 511

Strikeouts: Nolan Ryan – 5,076

Earned Run Average: Ed Walsh – 1.82

Hits per 9 Innings: Nolan Ryan – 6.57

TEAM RECORDS

Double Plays: Philadelphia Athletics, 1949 – 217

Wins: Chicago Cubs, 1906 – 116

Stolen Bases: New York Giants, 1911 – 347

Home Runs: Baltimore Orioles, 1996 – 257

World Series Appearances: New York Yankees – 34

World Championships: New York Yankees – 23

FURTHER READING

Dickey, Glenn. *History of the World Series Since 1903*. New York: Stein & Day, 1984.

Ivor-Campbell, Frederick, ed. *Baseball's First Stars*. Cleveland: Society for American Baseball Research, 1966.

Macht, Norman L. *Babe Ruth*. Philadelphia: Chelsea House Publishers, 1991.

Ward, Geoffrey C. and Ken Burns. *Baseball*. New York: Alfred A. Knopf, 1994.

White, G. Edward. *Creating the National Pastime*. Princeton, NJ: Princeton University Press, 1966.

INDEX

PICTURE CREDITS Library of Congress: pp. 2, 12, 17, 18, 23, 29, 54; Transcendental Graphics: pp. 6, 10; Patrick Morley: p. 14; National Archives: pp. 15, 38, 59; Boston Public Library: pp. 21, 24, 27, 31, 36, 43, 46; AP/Wide World: p. 34; New York Public Library: p. 22; UPI/Corbis-Bettmann: pp. 40, 50; National Baseball Library and Archives, Cooperstown, NY: pp. 49, 52, 56, 58, 60

NORMAN L. MACHT is the author of more than 25 books, 20 of them for Chelsea House Publishers. He is also the coauthor of biographies of former ballplayers Dick Bartell and Rex Barney, and is a member of the Society for American Baseball Research. He is the president of Choptank Syndicate, Inc. and lives in Baltimore, Maryland.